THE SUCCESSFUL REBEL

Getting What You Want
Without Losing Who You Are

Tracey Cox with Melissa Ireland

Most Trafford titles are also available at major online book retailers.

Note for Librarians: A cataloguing record for this book is available from Library
and Archives Canada at www.collectionscanada.ca/amicus/index-e.html

Printed in Victoria, BC, Canada.

ISBN: 978-1-4251-8654-8(sc)

Trafford rev. 9/18/2009

Trafford PUBLISHING® www.trafford.com

North America & international
toll-free: 1 888 232 4444 (USA & Canada)
phone: 250 383 6864 ♦ fax: 250 383 6804 ♦ email: info@trafford.com

The United Kingdom & Europe
phone: +44 (0)1865 487 395 ♦ local rate: 0845 230 9601
facsimile: +44 (0)1865 481 507 ♦ email: info.uk@trafford.com

10 9 8 7 6 5 4 3 2 1

For everyone who feels they are different and that they don't belong.

To our Successful Rebels and everyone on the way there.

Let your freak flag fly.

-- Tracey & Melissa

Acknowledgements

The authors would like to express our admiration and gratitude to all of the wonderful people who have made this book possible. In no particular order, we would like to thank Ville Valo, Ernie Boch Jr., Daemon and Raven Rowanchilde, Neev, Sloan Bella, Bart Smit, Alex and Allyson Grey, Mark Sanborn, Christina Cox, Bill Jamieson, Ariellah, James Ireland, Danielle Batone, Kari Valo, Taina Franzen, Ab and Marion Cox, Lloyd and Alexander Pope, Gina Spitzer and Charlotte Ireland for giving so much hope and love just by showing up.

A Special Note From Your Authors

The ideas presented in this book are not advice; they are observations on what makes a Successful Rebel.

We encourage you to follow your own heart, make your own decisions and find your own form of Successful Rebellion.

Question everything and everyone, including us.

Contents

FOREWORD

When my sister, Tracey Cox, approached me to work on "The Successful Rebel" I had a few worries. Who was I to advise potential rebels? I don't have a single tattoo or piercing and I have never considered myself a tortured artist. Yes I'd spent years in writers groups, went to arts school, tried my hand at the film biz, but I still felt curiously part of the mainstream.

It seemed a bit disingenuous to involve myself in the project when I wasn't obviously someone people would classify as a rebel.

Upon reflection, it occurred to me that it was this exact preconception of what a rebel is that needed to be addressed: rebellion isn't simply what you wear, what you say or who you hang out with. Being a rebel is about being true to yourself, and not being taken off your path by the myriad of detractors who want you to stay exactly as you have been, even if that isn't working for you. Being a rebel is understanding what makes you tick, even if that isn't popular, and finding a way to honor that in your unique way, within the society in which you live. A Successful Rebel doesn't become a hermit, or hide from life, spontaneously combust or drive those around them away. A Successful Rebel figures out the game and learns the rules so that he or she can challenge or break them. A Successful Rebel always knows who they are.

It takes courage to be authentic to yourself and to stay on the path you've chosen. To me, that is the true spirit of rebellion — "this doesn't work for me and I'm going to change it." No drama, no wasted energy, no raging against a "machine of unknown origin" – just being and then doing without worrying about a reaction. By this definition, Gandhi was a rebel, so was Galileo, Newton, Marx, Lincoln, Einstein, Picasso, Trudeau, and in our own time, Obama.

But perhaps the most important reason I decided to work on the book with Tracey was my desire to see people pursue their dreams, their unique identity without fear of recrimination or judgment. I've always wondered what makes people tick, who their best selves are, and how they can get there. It's something that I've investigated extensively in my own life and I hope that with that compassion and hard fought open mindedness we can help you see what makes a Successful Rebel.

One of the most memorable experiences of my life was when I attended Burning Man in 2003. I was part of "Acknowledgement Camp" which was formed of "Acknowledgement Angels". We stood in a booth; two at a time, with giant, gorgeous angel wings on and listened to what people wanted to be acknowledged for. It was an incredible experience watching people move from suspicion – "what do you want from me?" to false modesty "I haven't done that much" to total release when they felt completely acknowledged. I was struck by just how hard people are on themselves and how little credit we give others or ourselves in this life. When I asked individuals what they wanted to be acknowledged for, most couldn't come up with anything immediately, but with a bit of gentle prodding the most amazing stories poured forward: support for a dying partner, nursing an ailing parent, saving someone from a drug overdose... it was astounding. That these same people didn't think it was worth acknowledgement made me feel both sad and hopeful all at the same time.

If we can just see what we're all going through and acknowledge that pain and struggle, we can open ourselves up to the kind of life we've all dreamed of: compassion, love, understanding and freedom for all.

With love, Melissa Ireland, March 1, 2009

INTRODUCTION

Freaks, rebels, outcasts; there's a growing legion of us out there in the world. We don't want to swallow the pat answers that have been handed to us for so long. We are looking for a way to embrace success in our lives, without giving up who we are or what we believe in. We want a life of plenty, but on our own terms. The suit, the buttoned down corporate culture is not for us; we lust for freedom. We revel in our differences, and when we see others like us, we are drawn to them. We want to learn from others like ourselves, from our own tribe, to make our wildest dreams come true.

This book is for all of us, so that one day we can take positions of leadership in the world, and help shape it into a more tolerant place. To make it a better place for our children, so that they don't have to try and force themselves into the mould that has made us so miserable. So that we can save the planet and save ourselves at the same time; working together to throw off the chains of reliance on big business, big oil and the old boy network that has controlled things for so long. The planet needs a change, and we believe that the time has come for the rise of the rebel.

Tracey: I come from a long line of rebels. My great grandfather was a turn-of-the-century daredevil in the Barnum and Bailey Circus. On the other side of my family, my great grandfather opened the first Ford dealership in Oshawa, Ontario, which is a General Motors factory town. So I come by my nature honestly. I'm currently the General Manager of a well-respected domestic car dealership, and serve on the board of directors of a multimillion-dollar automotive corporation, but I've never fit into the corporate mould. I'm a comparatively young woman with tattoos, who loves alternative music, heavy eyeliner and classic cars. I tend to speak my mind, which can get me into trouble.

Throughout my life, I was always drawn to the rebels, and the successful people that operated outside of the box. Over the years I've collected friends and associates that were the same, but I've always noticed that there isn't much out there in terms of support or advice for us rebels. My theory on this is that within the makeup of a rebel is the tendency to avoid groups, as we've been shunned, excluded, or personally disgusted by so many. The very nature of a rebel includes a large portion of the lone wolf, so we can be very difficult to bring together, and even more difficult to organize. To move forward in our lives and truly manifest success for ourselves, I believe that we rebels need to mobilize and join forces to create an alternative template for success that all the young freaks, rebels and outcasts can look to and utilize as they make their way in the world. The alternative crowd needs to raise its voice and have a say in the coming age.

Alternative living, alternative medicine, alternative energy and alternative fuel. We hear about these every day in the media, but where is the support for the alternative people? In this book I have interviewed a diverse collection of Successful Rebels that have crafted their lives outside of the box, and I believe the world is a far richer place because of them. It is my hope that we can all learn from their words and be inspired by their stories. There are rebels out there that have made their dreams come true, and I believe that once we stop judging ourselves and using the measuring stick of the establishment, we will find true happiness and fulfillment in our alternative, rebellious, meaningful lives.

Melissa: Although not as easily identifiable as a "rebel" as my co-writer, I have long since decided to listen to inner wisdom, rather than following a prescribed set of plans to achieve success. I've had many different jobs, and even more dreams. I've lived in far flung locations because I decided it was the right thing to do for me. I've left perfectly good jobs because I needed a change – and I've eschewed the trappings of a "traditional" life in order to be as true to myself as I can be. Am I always successful? No, but each day I live with the comfort (and sometimes the consternation) that the path I've carved out for my life was my choice alone. Sometimes it works, and sometimes it doesn't, but I know in my heart that I haven't sold out.

This is what we want for you – to find your true, authentic self, and have the "rebelliousness" to stay true to that vision of yourself, without being swayed by pressures from friends, family or society in general.

The most liberating part of the current economic (and soon to be societal) meltdown is that it has become clear that there isn't one "right" way to do things, and that in fact those that have "toed the line" and "made the right choices" have been those worst affected.

The time is now to cast off the shackles and be who you are, without regret. Let us show you those that have done this and are happy and successful enough to share their stories with you. We owe them a big thank you for allowing us to interview them, and by way of introduction, here's a brief overview of our Successful Rebels.

∞

Ville Valo is the front man, lead singer and songwriter for the Finnish alternative rock band, HIM. HIM is the first Finnish band to receive a gold record in the United States and to date, the band has sold more than five and a half million albums worldwide. Ville is also the creator of the Heartagram, which is an intertwined heart and pentagram, and is the symbol for HIM. Often misunderstood, the Heartagram symbolizes the different aspects of love, and is seen emblazoned on the shirts and jackets of HIM fans worldwide. Most recently, Ville provided the voice of Moto Moto, the amorous hippo in the Finnish version of Disney's Madagascar 2: Escape to Africa. For more information on Ville Valo and HIM, please visit their website at Heartagram.com.

Sloan Bella is a gifted psychic medium, astrologer and metaphysician who has been featured on numerous television shows, and is a regular on the Montel Williams show. She is often employed by various police departments in the United States and Canada for help with missing persons and murder cases. Sloan has a large roster of celebrity clients, which reads like a who's who of Hollywood. She lives in the beautiful Verdugo Mountain area of Burbank with her husband and two young sons. For more information on Sloan, please visit her website at Sloanbella.com.

Ernie Boch Jr. is the number one Honda dealer and the number three Toyota dealer in America. He is also the most outrageous marketer in the automotive industry today, and what he does works. Check out his website Savearockstar.com and you'll see what we mean. Ernie is also an actor, playing the fire chief in Denis Leary's series "Rescue Me" and the leader of the band "Ernie and the Automatics", which he formed with two former members of the band Boston. We have long been admirers of Ernie and his antics, and if you'd like to see him in action, just enter his name in the search engine at YouTube, and enjoy. Ernie is an inspiration to every rebel that wants to let his freak flag fly and do things differently. For Ernie Boch Jr., the road less traveled has been the path to fame and fortune. For more information on Ernie, please visit his website at Boch.com.

Daemon Rowanchilde began tattooing in 1983, before attending and completing a program in Experimental and Fine Art at the Ontario College of Art in Toronto. Daemon studied Experimental Art, sculpture and jewelry design to loosen up his creativity and stimulate his imagination, and Fine Art to learn discipline and how to portray the human form in various media. It was during his time at OCA that Daemon developed the idea of tattooing as body design. He was fascinated by the dynamics of the human body in motion and how these dynamics could be enhanced by a skillfully placed and well-executed design. Today, Daemon's art and body design explore universal energy patterns perceived by shamans and reflected in the art and healing rituals of diverse cultures across time and space. He has done tattoos for Angelina Jolie and Billy Bob Thornton, and designed the tribal tattoos for Alan Cummings' character in X Men. His wife Raven Rowanchilde is his partner in business and life. She is a certified yoga instructor and energy worker, and they offer classes and workshops at their beautiful historic retreat in Fergus, Ontario. For more information, please visit their website at Urbanprimitive.com.

Bart Smit is an internationally acclaimed spiritual educator and deep trance channeler with a celebrity roster of clients. For over 20 years, Hollywood celebrities, British rock royalty and people from all walks of life have all benefited immensely from their sessions with Bart. Because he spends so much time in trance, he experiences different states of consciousness and has gained a wealth of knowledge about subtle states. Dr. Williams, who is channeled by Bart, serves as Bart's teacher and beloved mentor, has guided him and helped him to understand these subtle realms. Dr. Williams is pure consciousness and has been liberated from the cycle of birth and death. Through personal study and Dr. William's teachings, Bart has come to a deep understanding of the psychological characteristics of the chakras and the dance of inner liberation. For more information on Bart Smit, please see his website at bart-smit.com.

Alex Grey is a visionary artist, based in New York City, where his stunning gallery, the Chapel of Sacred Mirrors is located. Known and respected worldwide for the meditative quality of his paintings, Alex has painted the album covers for Tool, The Beastie Boys and Nirvana's In Utero. In 2009, Alex and his wife Allyson will be moving the Chapel to a picturesque estate outside of New York City, and reclaiming the land to return it to its pure state as an undertaking of radical eco art. For more information on Alex Grey and his Chapel of Sacred Mirrors, please visit his website at AlexGrey.com.

Neev is the founder and director of CALM, The Toronto Freedom Festival and The Global Marijuana March. CALM stands for Cannabis As Living Medicine, and it legally distributes medicinal marijuana to chronically ill patients in Canada. Neev is a tireless crusader for the legalization of cannabis, and the rights of the chronically ill to have access to this ancient therapy. For more information, please visit Cannabisclub.ca or Torontofreedomfestival.com.

Billy Jamieson is a classic rebel. He is a modern-day treasure hunter, an ancient and tribal arts collector and dealer. Part P.T. Barnum, part Indiana Jones, he searches the world for these oddities and curiosities and the historical stories behind them. Billy established an international reputation as a dealer and collector. His collection boasts an eclectic variety of ethnographic material, including shrunken human heads and war trophy skulls, weaponry, ancient Egyptian and Peruvian mummies, and a very unique collection of curiosities. In 1999 Billy purchased the entire contents of the Niagara Falls Museum, Canada's oldest museum, which opened in 1827. The collection included nine unidentified Egyptian mummies. While negotiating the deal, Billy and Egyptologists began an investigation, which would eventually lead to one of these mummies being identified as the missing Egyptian Pharaoh Ramses I. Billy sold the nine mummies to the Michael C. Carlos museum, which is part of Emery University in Atlanta, Georgia, where the ID was confirmed. Ramses I was then returned to Egypt and is now on display at the Luxor Museum. Today Billy owns and operates William Jamieson Ancient and Tribal Art from his Toronto studio; a cross between a museum, and an art deco/gothic mansion. He works regularly with major auction houses such as Sotheby's and Christie's, and has sold and donated fine works of art to the Royal Ontario Museum, New York Metropolitan Museum, The Houston Museum of Fine Art, The Indiana State Museum and many private collectors. Billy is also a member of the Canadian Chapter of the New York Explorers Club and holds annual events as his home.

Although Billy is largely self-educated, he has become respected for his growing expertise as an Ethnologist Museoligist. He has also financed five expeditions into the jungles of Ecuador and Peru, at times visiting the Shuar tribe, among other cultures. He is also a sought-after lecturer and is often called upon to give tours of his museum/home. He is an explorer, adventurer, and art dealer with a rock and roll sensibility. Bill lists Mick Jagger, Steven Tyler, Getty Lee, Danny Elfman, Jonathan Davis, Tim Burton, and Nikki Sixx among his many celebrity visitors. For more information on Bill Jamieson, please visit his website at jamiesontribalart.com, egyptianmuseum.com, niagaramuseum.com and explorersclub.ca.

Mark Sanborn is the president of Sanborn & Associates, an idea lab for leadership development. Leadershipgurus.net lists Mark as one of the top 15 leadership experts in the world. In addition to his experience leading at an international level, he has written and co-authored 7 books, and is the author of more than two dozen audio and video training programs on leadership, change, teamwork and customer service. Mark is a member of the prestigious Speakers Roundtable, 20 of the top speakers in the world today, and is also a member of the Speakers Hall of Fame. Mark's book *The Fred Factor: How Passion In Your Work and Life Can Turn the Ordinary Into the Extraordinary* is an international bestseller and was on the New York Times, Business Week and Wall Street Journal bestseller lists. His newest books are *You Don't Need a Title to Be a Leader: How Anyone, Anywhere Can Make a Positive Difference*, and *The Encore Effect: How to Achieve Remarkable Performance in Anything You Do*. Mark is a past president of the

National Speakers Association and Winner of the Cavett Award. For more information please visit MarkSanborn.com.

Christina Cox stars as Jen Crane in the upcoming Fox Television Studios series "Defying Gravity". Christina's career began with her Gemini nominated performance as Angie Ramirez in "FX: The Series" and she most recently starred in Lifetime's cult favorite "Blood Ties". Her film roles include "The Chronicles of Riddick" and "Better than Chocolate" among others, as well as recurring roles and guest stars on shows such as "House", "Bones", "Cold Case", and "CSI Miami."

So, without further ado, let's meet our Successful Rebels…

PART 1

Chapter 1:
Internal Revolution:
Rebellion Starts At Home

"Disobedience, in the eyes of anyone who has read history, is man's original virtue. It is through disobedience that progress has been made, through disobedience and through rebellion."

- Oscar Wilde

Tracey: I guess that my reasons for beginning this journey were fairly selfish. I had been going through some very challenging times in my business and I thought that if I could speak to some of the rebels that I have greatly admired, they might give me some advice to help me understand how to operate more successfully, and more authentically. The typical success books that I've read in the past just don't resonate with me. They tend to be more geared towards the "suits", and I am definitely not one of them. As I began to speak to these people, the information that they were sharing was so motivating and inspiring, I knew that I had to get the word out to other rebels like me.

The first interview that I did was with the Finnish musician, Ville Valo. Ville is the front man, lead singer and songwriter for the Finnish alt rock band, HIM. His band has been going strong for over thirteen years, and has sold more than five and a half million copies of their albums worldwide. Better known everywhere else on the planet than in North America, Ville hopes to change that very soon. I certainly hope that the North American market opens up for them in the manner that they deserve. HIM is a fantastic band. Ville Valo's music is like the feeling that you get right before the first kiss, the first touch of love; the highest anticipation of ecstasy, in sonic form.

Being a longtime admirer of the man and his music, I was fairly nervous when I called Ville in his tower in Helsinki. His warm and friendly manner put me immediately at ease however, and I found myself speaking to him as I would an old friend. When I first asked him if his assistant had filled him in on why I was interviewing him, he responded "I saw bits and pieces, so I kind of know what's going on… but it's also that I don't want to know too much in advance… that way I don't obliviously start formulating stupid answers to wise questions." I was impressed by Ville Valo from the start of my conversations with him, and over the hours that he generously shared with me, he never disappointed.

I began our interview by giving Ville some background about why I was interviewing him and writing this book. I told him that what I'm trying to do with this subject matter is empower the rebels, because we need to have a voice in what's going on in the world right now.

Tracey: There's been so much marginalization of people that are a little bit fringy, and I'm trying to get the word out that it's okay to be individuals, it's okay to be different, it should be embraced, actually.

Ville: Oh yeah, well, tell that to the schooling systems. I'm fairly sure that this generation or the next one, I think we're going to end up with a generation with no artists. All the artists are a bit fucked up… in the head or in the heart, and the modern system just shoves down a lot of ADD symptoms on those kids, and shoves down a lot of pills. And everybody seems to have some kind of diagnosis of Asperger's syndrome or whatever.

Ville Valo. Photo credit: Jarmo Katila

Tracey: Let me give you a bit of background on me and my experiences, so that you know where I'm coming from. I was raised to be a feminist. My parents, especially my mother were always very into the idea of equality, whether it be about race or sex. I was raised in a General Motors factory town, and my family has been in the car business for almost a hundred years, so me and my sisters were expected to pull our weight in whatever needed to be done, whether it was a traditionally male or female task, it really didn't matter. We were raised to think that women could do anything that men could do.

Ville: So that's what feminism means for you. It's not burning up bras and claiming ladies to be better than men?

Tracey: No, no… not claiming better, claiming equal.

Ville: *laughs* Well, that's obvious that ladies are equal, and actually a bit more, I guess.

Tracey: Well, that's sweet that you think so, but I think that we have to take each person on their own merits.

Ville: Fair enough, yeah. At the end of the day, I do forget…I should concentrate here…and you know, I'm a desperate heterosexual in need of some companionship, so I'm very willing and able to go fairly far forward in my feminism. I understand women's anger at not being taken seriously.

Throughout the interview, Ville had a very relaxed way of relating, and he really made me laugh. At the same time, he had a very interesting way of cutting to the heart of the matter. I began to tell him the story of where I felt that my rebellion in life first began.

Tracey: When I was seven, the principal of my school used to come into our class and announce, "I need five boys to come down to the book room and carry books up for the classes." And to me, I thought that was real discrimination towards women, and I was very militant at that age. One day I had finally had enough, so I stood up to the principal and said, "Why do you always have to have the boys carry the books? We girls are just as big and strong, and it's discrimination." And from that time forward, my life in school was hell. I had questioned him, and he made out that there was something wrong with me, mentally. I was set up with the school psychologist. Well, it turned out that he was molesting the boys down in that book room, and it was a big case here in Canada, all over the news. The guy made my life a living hell, because he thought I was on to him. And the school psychologist was only questioning me to see if I knew anything, which of course I didn't. I don't think that the psychologist knew that this evil man was using him, he was just doing his job, and I was just a little girl, expressing my outrage about sexual discrimination.

Ville: Oh my God. It sounds like a detective novel. Thank God you weren't a boy.

Tracey: That's for sure. But what I'm getting at is there are so many children that are victimized in this way for being different, and the problem is that it's not so much about them and what they're doing, it's about the adult that's dealing with them. It's odd living your life that way, when you know that there's something different about you, and it's being put on you as your responsibility. The powers that be are trying to tell you that there's something wrong with you, instead of them supporting you as an individual. It made public school a hellish place for me.

Ville: Being in the public school where I was, at least, back here, the thing basically is that I don't necessarily think that the most important thing that you learn through school is the history, or the language. The lesson you learn is to live amongst people that you don't necessarily like. Because you know, that's the way of the world, you have to be able to find a way to cope because you know when you grow up you have to learn to work with people that you maybe don't dislike, but you don't want to spend your free time with either. So in that sense, getting to know the social rules in a way, and to learn how to work as a team, is very essential when it comes to school, but yes I do think that a lot of places tend to drag the sensitivity and the poetic soul out of a kid very easily, and make the youth very jaded before they actually have the right to become jaded.

Tracey: That's right, but being jaded develops within a child because of these types of situations. They lose faith in the world. In your experience, when you were growing up, did you know people that were rebels, but that were successful as well? Because a lot of the time the character trait that brought them the most torment as they grew up was actually the key to their success later on in life. Is there anything that caused you that torment, but has actually translated into what has brought you success?

Ville: Well, I think it's more about internal torment. When I was in a school, I was fairly hyper active and my parents were really worried, as I was trying to be the king of the hill, and getting into a lot of fights, and things like that. I wasn't bad in school, I was attending all the classes, and I wasn't doing that bad, but my parents were really worried about me, and they were talking to my teacher. My teacher was a wise old lady, and I think that unfortunately she's passed away, as I haven't been able to locate her, but she said "don't worry about it, all great artists are like that when they're young." So that was her attitude. And you know, I don't know how great of an artist I've become, but it was really easy going in that sense. I got into a lot of trouble, but I loved Finnish language, mathematics, and I had really tough teachers, and everything in between, and I had to learn how to live amongst the sheep. So nobody tried to kill my creativity, quite the opposite, they gave me a special right to be able to draw in class. I wasn't able to concentrate, so I needed to do something with my hands, so I was drawing all the time. During all the classes, and it was never a big problem. I think that the rest of the kids thought that it was a bit kooky, but I didn't have a problem with that.

Tracey: But it didn't bother you…their judgment didn't affect you one way or another, or did it?

Ville: Not really, no, and after a couple of years I was able to attend a class that was a bit more into the arts, and we had a lot of kooky children in the school, so I was able to do that, so in that sense I'm quite the contrary to the traditional rebelling kid. I never had the opportunity of breaking out of the shell until later in life, through sex, drugs and rock and roll. I was basically able to do all that when I was 13, because I was already playing in the clubs and not for the booze, but for the music and I was playing hard core music, and reggae, and then again I was playing jazz things, so you know, I had really quite the contrary experience. My dad at that time was a cab driver, and he said "do whatever you want to do, but don't become a cab driver." He really didn't want that life for me. You know, he and my mother bought me my first instruments, and they paid for my bass guitar lessons, and they were really supportive. My dad's a really great guy, but he never had the opportunity to study the arts, as he had to start working really young, and he was born in the late forties, and that was the time that it was tougher and rougher on kids that possibly had a little aspiring artist in them. There wasn't a lot of money around, and that was a struggle. In that sense I think that my dad missed out, and he didn't want to see the same thing happen to me, so he was really supportive. And I understand that is very rare, but you know, I didn't have anything besides music. And music was my only friend, and still is, to a certain extent. It's the mirror that I have, to try and understand what's going on in the world. I live through music, and I always have. It's a blessing and a curse.

Tracey: One of the things that stood out to me as I spoke to Ville was that the spirit of a child seems to express itself at an early age, and it's all about the way that the adults surrounding the child channel that spirit that defines whether the child's life is a triumph or a tragedy. Ville was blessed with parents and teachers that supported his so called "hyper activity", and channeled his energy into expressing his gift, which has given pleasure to so many of his fans. I, on the other hand, was persecuted for my feminist ideals that I expressed in school. The principal that I mentioned earlier (who ended up in jail for his monstrous behavior) actually called my mother into school one day to complain to her that I only played with the boys. He used it as an accusation, that there was something untoward that was going on; even though I was just a little girl whose best friends were male. My mother got into a fight with him and stood up for me. My "playing with the boys" was actually a blessing, as a woman in the automotive business, I need to be tough and deal with men on their own level. Early rebellion is an expression of spirit, and how it is nurtured is the responsibility of all adults in a position of authority.

Melissa: I had an easy time in school. I actually liked it. Legend has it that I was pleading to go to school with my older sister when I was only 3 years old. I liked to draw, I liked to read, and I liked to be busy. So I didn't really have any "behavioral" issues that resulted in calls home, but I was victimized just the same. One on my most vivid memories came when I was only twelve years old. I was blossoming in more ways than one and it was really tough being the only girl in the school with substantial breasts! To be honest, I hated them, and did everything I could to hide them. I'd experienced creepy men in shopping malls trying to pick me up, catcalls, and boys "talking to my chest" and frankly anything that smacked of female sexuality seemed like a righteous pain in the ass to me. Now, as a mature woman, my views of this have changed, but I still dress in boxier and more masculine clothes than I probably should. But that's a topic for another book.

This particular memory springs from a public speaking competition when I was in grade six. I loved public speaking, because I liked ideas: forming them and expressing them. It also made me feel good to get up and perform my own material. It was somewhere between acting and music for me. I'd made it to the finals, and it was down to me and another classmate, and he won. Naturally I was disappointed, but not as upset as I would become when I heard what one of the judges had said to my mother. This woman, old enough to know better, a teacher no less, told my mother that although I had lost "I shouldn't worry too much – that I was so pretty I wouldn't need to work that hard in life anyway." This was in 1980, folks!

That statement scorched me more than any loss ever could have. Somehow, I didn't "need" to win, because she figured I'd already won the genetic lottery and didn't need any more help. My form of rebellion was quite clear – I cast off any sense of the feminine I could – I needed to be taken seriously! It was a perfectly rational response to a totally irrational statement and it's one that I struggle with to this day. Words can be powerful, and we need to watch how we talk to our children and ourselves.

Sloan Bella knows all too well how damaging and discouraging it can be to grow up without feeling supported and loved. Sloan is a professional psychic medium, based in Hollywood, with an impressive list of celebrity clients. When we spoke with Sloan, she opened up and shared a heartbreaking tale of a truly tough childhood.

Tracey: From the research that I've done, it seems common to Successful Rebels that the character trait that brought them the most torment as they grew up was actually the key to their success later on in life. Do you think that there's anything like that in your makeup?

Sloan: I have no idea what the others think, but for myself, absolutely. For me personally, it was the distress within our household. And the fact of feeling uprooted through being adopted. Knowing that you're an adopted child. I always knew, they made a point of telling me. I think that the agency told my parents to tell me. I remember noticing in the mirror that I didn't look like them. Other than the fact that we're all white, I don't look like them. At that point, I was probably about the age of three or four, I noticed that I was different looking. I smelled different, I looked different, and I remember thinking that. I remember looking in the mirror at my face and thinking "who is this?" I knew I had a mother and father, obviously, but it was very clear in our family that I was adopted. That was always brought into conversations. "Well, you're adopted." The adopted sister, the adopted child. This is our adopted daughter. It's never, "this is our daughter". So that's a way to make a child feel like an outcast right away. That's how I felt. Adopted. When you know what that means, once you get past that element of it, you wonder why your "real" mother didn't keep you. Unfortunately, that's the ego talking because we think that we're special. In the grand scheme of things, nobody's special. We're all equal. Homeless, famous, whatever. It doesn't matter, we're all equal. Therefore, people make choices that fulfill their needs and not yours. But a child doesn't know that. I had no idea of that. I thought that my mother must have been a terrible person, because she gave me up. So always thinking about her out there somewhere, what was she doing, what did she look like, and adding that to the chaos within our family, alcoholism on my father's part for example. It made me want to prove to them and myself that I didn't need them. Because I figured that, being adopted, I didn't want to have to need them, because they might give me up too. That was my mindset. I don't need you, you can't affect me.

Three months after I turned fourteen, I ran away from home. November 13th. I still remember. I left King City and ran away to downtown Newmarket (Ontario, Canada). Not the brightest of all things, but then I moved to downtown Toronto after that. And I was working with my psychic ability, doing astrology the whole time. When I was very young, about seven years old, I started learning about astrology. I can remember when it hit in my head. I can remember when my light bulb went off. I got a birthday gift from my aunt in England, and she sent me an astrology necklace. The strange thing was that it wasn't my proper sign, it was a Scorpio and I'm a Leo. She didn't think it was a problem, but I felt that she had sent me size 10 shoes, when I was a 7. It didn't hit me as being right, but it sparked my interest, and I started to learn about it. That's when I started doing the astrology. The psychic stuff was a constant, from day one. I remember at the age of four thinking that God was talking to me. And that's not good when you're adopted, because they call you crazy. I was never raised religiously, we never went to church. But these voices would tell me things, and tell me to tell my father. His dead relatives would come through and ask me to give him these messages, and even though they were valid points, he would become enraged. That type of thing doesn't usually work with alcoholics. I would constantly try to give him these messages, and I would get in big trouble. It was a nightmare. I would hear them whispering to themselves, and they would be saying, "she's right, but she's crazy!"

∞

Daemon Rowanchilde began tattooing in 1983, before attending and completing a program in Experimental and Fine Art at the Ontario College of Art in Toronto. His celebrity clients include such A list stars as Angelina Jolie and Billy Bob Thornton. Daemon is considered a pioneer in the Tribal style of tattooing.

Tracey: Do you feel that you have a character trait that gave you strength as an adult, but was a source of torment as a child?

Daemon: Well, I was a very sensitive child and I went through a lot of child abuse from my father. But I didn't acknowledge what was happening. I think that a lot of children do that to make the person right who's actually wrong, just to make things make sense to a child's mind. So you bend to accommodate their bullshit, so that went against me, but in that happening, my creativity flourished. Suffering does produce the artistic condition. I went through some really hyperactive times of creation as a way to deal. Most of the time I was pretty average, you know a little bit sensitive, a little bit self conscious at times, shy person, but later on in life through doing a lot of psychedelic explorations I surfaced a whole bunch of shit that was underneath and that surfaced as insomnia and hyperactivity. It was like, fuck, where the hell is this shit coming from? Okay, now you have to deal with your past. Then through things like tinkering with my own TV set because no one else was figuring it out for me, I learned about reality and how it worked. And my studies in Buddhism and everything else, I mean I studied every spiritual path and it caused me to learn about myself. At that time I thought I was fixing myself, but later on I realized that I wasn't broken to begin with, it was my belief system that was broken, and all I had to do was let go. And through that great struggle came great beauty.

Tracey: It's like that saying: the North wind made the Viking. That's why I'm trying to do this book. I want the rebels and freaks to have a resource. You can be questing, and interested, and wondering about death, and a geek and a nerd and a rebel and a really cool person, and you can want to find out these answers, but don't beat yourself up feeling like you're a screw-up or that things are going badly. Rebels and freaks are too hard on themselves.

Daemon: Society has created a template that gives the idea that there is a norm and anything outside that is a freak. And that template doesn't exist…it's fake. As soon as the template dissolves, the freak dissolves. And you just are who you are. And you stop trying to fit in. But the stuff beyond trying to fit is trying to fight it. At some point you have to let go of trying to fight it and just become yourself. That is true liberation.

Daemon was able to channel his tremendous artistic talent into an area that made sense to him, which has resulted in a steady stream of high end clients, a thriving business, a beautiful retreat in the country, and perhaps most importantly, knowledge that he is living his true life. Fighting takes a lot of energy and as Daemon has correctly pointed out; you can only become yourself when you put the sword down and just be.

Ernie Boch Jr., our rebel entrepreneur always had a sense of the outrageous.

Tracey: One of the things that I'm finding in a lot of my research is that most Successful Rebels like yourself seem to have a character trait that when they were growing up, it made things difficult for them in some ways, like they got teased or tormented about it at some point, but it actually turned out to be a key to their success. Was there anything like that when you were growing up?

Ernie: Well, yeah, I would think that yes, I was on TV doing a commercial in 1968, you know, when I was 10 years old, and you know, I got a lot of flak from my friends for doing that.

Tracey: With your dad the car dealer, you mean?

Ernie: I was actually by myself. It was his commercial, but I was by myself at ten, on the air.

Tracey: Oh, really? So you had it going on real early!

Ernie: Yeah, and as a matter of fact, that summer, or maybe the summer after, I think it was 1969 or 70, that musical Hair, it toured across the country and in a certain section of that musical they would take local things from the city and comment on them. Well, during that play, they would talk about this and that, one girl gets up and says "My hero's Ernie Boch Jr.!" and faints! And they did that at the Wilbur Theatre, with all the local people in the audience.

Tracey: That's amazing! Great promo for the dealership! So, you got teased for some of the stuff that you did as a child, but obviously, look how that turned out! But you're also a musician, correct? And that's still a big part of your life?

Ernie: Yeah, for sure. I think that music brings me my biggest happiness and my biggest rewards, personally I mean.

∽∞

Christina Cox had a deep sense of being "other" as a child.

Tracey: It seems to be common to everybody that I have spoken with, the character trait that brought them the most torment as they grew up was actually the key to the successes that they've had later on in life. Do you feel that there's anything like that for you?

Christina: Well, I don't know what anyone else's "things" are but one thing I often encounter with other actors is that they're either the eldest or the baby of the family. I don't see a lot of middle children. The eldest has a very clear opinion of who they are, as they got the most attention, the most focused attention before the parents were exhausted and they have a strong sense of self. Alternately, the baby arrives and everyone is sort of wrung out and the baby is jumping up and down and saying "Hey, I'm over here, I exist!" and is trying desperately to be seen. Ultimately, just jumping up and down and saying "hey, hey, hey", never really gets you anywhere, so you start to be funny. Or you start to be endearing. Or cute. Or putting on little shows. People will watch and then you begin getting attention and affirmation that you exist. That you are seen. I can understand that with young parents, they may be a little tired by the time they get to number three or four! In my case added to that was a house with some really strong personalities…I mean, you try being five and being heard at a dinner table with the lot of you, and it's hard work. Maybe that influenced my desire or strengthened my ability to break through and be seen, to have my voice heard.

The other thing for me is that I've always felt like such an outcast. Like such an outsider. I never felt that really settled in feeling of belonging at any of the schools that I went to. I didn't feel that I said the right things or wore the right things, and it didn't bother me, but I just was like "wow, I'm really not the same."

Tracey: It was an awareness.

Christina: Yeah. An awareness that I had no interest in "belonging" and that these people really don't know what the hell I'm talking about.

Tracey: I felt the same thing.

Christina: Yes, and at a certain point in high school, I just thought, "I'm going to stop trying." I didn't actually care what they were talking about. What was their favorite mascara, and who was going to make the volleyball team...I mean I was on the volleyball team, but the politics never occurred to me. Not that anyone was wrong, just different. I was also in a specialized dance and theatre program and I realized fitting in was going to be impossible so I stopped trying. And in that, good or bad, I kind of marginalized myself, which in retrospect has definitely affected the way that I interact with the world. But it also let me go "you know what, this is how I communicate with the world, and I communicate better through poetry or through writing or through performing". I was never going to be the prom queen, never be popular. But when I was on stage, suddenly I felt like I belonged and I also realized what a powerful effect theatre has on people. This ability to affect what people think and feel. I mean, I don't feel that actors are splitting the atom or curing disease by any means...but if it makes someone reconsider their point of view, or opens up new ideas...that's pretty amazing.

Tracey: No, of course, but your profession does have a lot of influence, especially in this age of celebrity fascination...

Christina: It just made me go, wow, along with the opportunity, there's a real responsibility here. Plus I really loved to do it although to be honest I loved dance more than acting, but for me it was not a realistic career because of injuries. I loved being on stage just throwing it all out there. The moments of purity and clarity, especially in television and film can be few and far between while you're working your way up. When they happen, they're brilliant and you go "oh God, this is why I'm in it", but that's one out of ten jobs, maybe are art, or vaguely like art. You can get some brilliant piece of writing and you end up with it last on the schedule, and they have 45 minutes to shoot it. You do your best, but the impact that having the time to light it properly and get enough coverage of it so that it can be edited together well. On Blood Ties Dylan Neal and I had so many great scenes together. I had such an amazing, positive experience doing the show with everyone but the reality was we had way too much to get done every day and it often meant coverage would get lost. There was this one great scene in the hallway, I think it was in the last episode and we ran out of time. This whole hugely emotional scene was pretty much shot in a profile two shot. How much emotion are you possibly going to capture in a profile shot? It still ended up great because Dylan is insanely good but I would love to have seen it with the coverage it deserved. But that's the reality of it and I'm so proud of the work we did. A good performance can be carved out of a mediocre actor because they have enough coverage and a skilled editor and a great performance can be lost from a good actor because they've only been able to shoot a master. Plus there are so many other things that have to come together, an alchemy that has to happen for a project to work. It felt that way on BT, just a little magic when Kyle and Dylan and Gina and I would get rolling and it reminded me a little of being on stage, whether it was dance or being in theatre, feeling that energetic response when you hit it, when you find that place that people go "ahh", and you know that they're in it, you know they've surrendered to it, and it's very powerful. It feels that way on "Defying Gravity", this little collective "Ooh, I think we may have something here" feeling, hopefully that will turn out to be true. I hope that I keep making choices that respect and support that intention. I know that I've made some goofy and less than stellar straight to video stuff, but you have to live, you have to pay the bills.

∞

Neev has been a fearless proponent for the legalization of medicinal marijuana – a calling that frequently puts him on the "wrong" side of the law.

Neev is the founder and director of CALM, The Toronto Freedom Festival and The Global Marijuana March. CALM stands for Cannabis As Living Medicine, and it legally distributes medicinal marijuana to chronically ill patients in Canada.

Tracey: Being in the automotive industry, I'm sometimes asked to provide unusual customizations and modifications to vehicles, and it was one of those requests that led me to my interview with Neev, the founder of CALM, and organizer of the Toronto Freedom Festival and the Global Marijuana March. Neev was looking for someone to build a hemp-fueled car for Tommy Chong to drive in the parade for the Toronto Freedom

Festival, and I had been researching alternative fuel conversions for classic cars for a few years. Mostly what I had been doing was listening to people in the industry telling me that "you can't do that, and here's why." Plenty of people with no imagination, and even more that didn't even want to think about the possibilities of eco conversions. This was about three years ago, and man, times have changed. Eco conversions, hybrids and electric cars are all anyone talks about in the industry now, but three years ago I had people look at me like I had two heads when I tried to source out any of these options. I still have a 67 Olds 442 Convertible filed away for an electric engine conversion, and I'm looking forward to that day.

Tracey: With everyone that I've talked to, it seems to be fairly common to rebels that have had some success, that the character trait that brought them the most torment as they grew up was actually the key to their success later on in life. Do you feel that there's anything like that in your life?

Robin (Neev's friend): Can I answer that? In my opinion, Neev's greatest strength and his greatest weakness is that he always follows his own path, and won't ever let anyone tell him what to do or what to think. And that can be insanely frustrating, but it's allowed him to do things that other people have thought were crazy, and they turn out to be successful. You could say to Neev that they sun rises in the east, and he will say to you, "but does it have to?"

Tracey: Did that give you problems as you grew up?

Neev: Well, I knew that I was smarter than most people…wait, that's not quite right. I'm not very smart, and I'm not very creative, but I'm a unique blend of both. I was never able to express myself very well; it was all in my head. I knew that I understood everything, I just couldn't express myself. As I got older that changed, and I decided to use my strengths to stand up for what I believed in.

Tracey: Were you considered an introvert in school?

Neev: Let's just say that I was not socially successful.

Another individual who has made a name for himself doing what came "unnaturally" is Bart Smit. Bart Smit is an internationally acclaimed spiritual educator and deep trance channeler with a celebrity roster of clients. When Bart goes into trance, he channels Dr. Williams. This kind hearted, funny, taskmaster calls you on all of your garbage and makes it impossible to hide. Your authors have both seen him for counsel and have never been disappointed. You always leave the sessions energized, if a bit embarrassed by your own hubris, and ready to take on the world. It is truly the most loving, no nonsense hour you'll ever spend with a complete stranger.

Tracey: I'm trying to reach out to people that feel that they don't fit in, feel like they aren't heard, and want to be successful but want to do it in their own way. What message would you like to get out to those people to give them a little bit of hope or spur them on so that they can make it happen for themselves? Words of wisdom?

Dr. Williams: The first stage within revolution is that we are different from everyone else. If we could recognize this, then we are on the first step of moving towards our destiny. The second step is to realize that we are different, therefore we offer a different perspective. It is this perspective that the Universe is in need of. As long as we all follow the same path, we never reach a greater potential as individuals, because we're all traveling on the same highway, going in the same direction. Individuals that have the courage to get off the highway that leads in the same direction, and find new undiscovered, unknown territories are those that truly begin to live life to its fullest, because they are no longer within the mainstream of our society. Mainstream isn't right or wrong; it is limited. It is the most comfortable path for everyone to travel on. To be a great warrior, to discover new territory, is an individual that truly has discovered the deepest meaning of life.

Everyone we spoke to echoed this sentiment – yes – first of all you must recognize that you are different, and fight the good fight to have that recognized. But that is only the first stage of your development. If you continue to be stuck in the infantilized stage of rebellion you'll be nothing but a poser. Rebellion for rebellion's sake is as useless as pretending to be someone you're not. You're still not authentic and you're still not contributing.

In the following chapters, we'll discover the different stops along the ways, the pitfalls, the joys and the rewards.

In other words, "So you're a rebel. Now what?"

Chapter 2:
Blowing Smoke:
The Bullshit Detector

Perhaps the most important skill that any of us on the planet can develop is a nose for bullshit. What do we mean by this rather crude term? That which is inauthentic, untrue, false. At its best it is naiveté, blind faith, or ignorance. At its worst? Intolerance, bigotry and manipulation in its most powerful form.

So why is it important to be able to spot and dismiss bullshit? BS keeps us complacent. It distracts us from the truth. It keeps us stuck, believing our own press. It blows seven different kinds of smoke and has us stray from our true path.

Is everyone's definition of bullshit identical? No – one person's flattery is another's smoke.

Perhaps the litmus test is this – does it feel right to you? Or do you feel that you are being humored, cajoled, blown-off or otherwise dismissed? This doesn't mean you have carte blanche to simply dismiss opinions that don't match your own. It means you need to measure your reaction to your gut, your instincts and your intuition about the subject area at hand.

There is no quick route to this; it's as much a learned behavior as it is an instinct. Let's see what some of our Successful Rebels have done to develop this crucial talent.

Tracey: You know, just from my observations, a lot of the people that I've run into that are rebels or freaks, or whatever you want to call them, one of the common things that I'm finding with everybody is that they have a really highly developed bullshit detector. Do you know what I'm saying?

Where they can pick up on if people are lying, or full of it or hypocrites or that type of thing.

Ville: *laughs* Yeah, well, it kind of starts from "just don't trust anybody"!

Tracey: Do you think that you have that yourself? Do you think that you're pretty good at sniffing out the bullshit?

Ville: More or less, but at times, I do enjoy the bullshit…So, the bullshit is not necessarily a negative thing and it's actually cool to see good bullshitters do what they do! Because there are great bullshitters as well…great people talking bull, and I've been meeting a lot of people within the music industry, obviously I've met a lot of people who, you know, say different things and do other things, and so yeah, I don't have any problem with this. I've got my good, close friends and at the end of the day, I really don't trust too many people because people change, and their views change, and that's their right. You know, a lot of people share 30% of their secrets with one really close friend, 30% with somebody else, and 40% with somebody else, and maybe keeping some as a secret. That's what a lot of people do. Whether intentionally or not.

Tracey: A lot of the people outside of the norm, they can see through a lot of that stuff, a lot of the façade, a lot of the phoniness, and it's how they channel that knowledge that sets them apart as being successful. Or they self-destruct because they just rage against it and go right off the rails.

Ville: Yeah, I get it, but it's not too far from, let's say, you know, gay people coming out of the closet back in the day. Because, they do have the bullshit detector as well. I think even now in some cultures, it's a pretty sensitive topic, and it's a big thing for a person who's sure of what he or she wants, and to come clean about that thing to everybody. To society, to your parents, and especially in religious places, it's a big deal, so it means just coming clean about being different. In that sense, it's very similar to artists, or to freaks or rebels of any kind. By trying to prove yourself, you tend to meet a lot of people who say "yeah, yeah, yeah, I do understand what you're saying", but they really don't give a fuck.

So it really is about being able to see the truth – about looking through the world that we live in, and seeing, with compassion, the system that runs under everything. It's about having that understanding that all of us are projecting varying levels of our truthfulness and rather than getting pissed that someone is lying or deceiving, you just see it for what it is. And move on.

Let's meet Mark Sanborn, an outstanding motivational speaker and author.

Tracey: So, Mark, do you think you have a bullshit detector?

Mark: One of my potential weaknesses is that I don't suffer fools - or posers - gladly. By "fools" I don't mean people of low IQ, but rather people who aren't trying to think or apply themselves to living. Posers are those people who talk a much better game than they play. So I guess you would say that I have a pretty good BS detector.

Mark Sanborn

Also, I learned that the key is to be skeptical (questioning) without becoming cynical (angry and disengaged). I learned that to be successful we need to answer our questions and question our answers. Pat answers are usually unexamined answers; the quicker you come up with an answer, the less likely it is to be the best answer.

Melissa: I think what's key in Mark's response is the idea of questioning versus becoming resigned and cynical. Because let's face it folks, there will be times when you're wrong. If you keep an open heart and an open mind when you're running up against someone you think may be trying to shine you on, then at the very least you're going to learn something. At worst, you've spent a few minutes of your life trying to understand another human being.

∞

Christina Cox, an actor that has toiled in the extremely competitive world of film and television, has seen her share of ups and downs. She's starred in several series, several pilots and has even co-created and sold a pilot in which she would star. She's somewhat of a cult figure in both the sci-fi and gay community from her performances in "The Chronicles of Riddick" and "Better Than Chocolate" as well as "Nikki & Nora", a UPN pilot filmed in pre-Katrina New Orleans that has become one of the most-watched, never aired pilots in history. Her television appearances are too numerous to list, but it would be fair to call her a journeyman. At the time this book was written, Christina was about to embark on a new leading role in a highly anticipated new Fox Television Studios series, "Defying Gravity".

Tracey: Christina Cox and my co-author Melissa Ireland are both my sisters. Christina has always been an ass kicker of the first order. My earliest memories of her are as a daredevil and a protector. You really don't want to mess with her. She has a fierce protectiveness of her loved ones. Her martial arts and sword skills are second to none, and I think that she must have some of my great grandfather's daredevil blood running through her veins. One of the biggest problems growing up was controlling her when Melissa and I had to baby-sit her. If you took your eyes off of Christina, she was up to something crazy. Once on a trip to Las Vegas with the family, we looked up to the third floor balcony that ran around the pool, and Christina was walking around on top of the canopy that covered the walkway. On top. She was seven years old at the time. When we lived in Ottawa, we caught her jumping into the pool from our parent's second floor balcony. One time she came home from being downtown with her friends (she was about 13 at the time), and she was walking fairly gingerly. We eventually caught a glimpse of her side and it was completely torn up. It turned out that she and her friends were jumping from rooftop to rooftop in downtown Ottawa, and somehow Christina had missed, just barely held on to the ledge and had to pull herself up. Our parents only found out about that one last Christmas!! So it's no wonder that Christina Cox has been a successful actor who does a lot of her own stunts. She was born for it.

Tracey: I think that part of what you go through, and the torment that you deal with comes from the fact that you have the nature of a rebel, and I think that one of the biggest parts of the nature of a rebel is that they all have a highly developed bullshit detector. They also have an inability to swallow pat answers and a desire for true information, and they don't accept the status quo. I know that is part of what you've run up against. You can see through the bullshit. So, how do you use that and not use it, to make your ends happen? How to you turn it on and shut it off? How do you approach that?

Christina: Well, I think that you have to try and interact with people being as present as you can and handle them all with the same grace but be aware of the sharks and people who have ulterior motives. I've been pretty lucky as a woman in this business, my boundaries are so clear they tend to be wary of me compared to the experiences of some of the other women that I know. By the same token sometimes my having such defined boundaries for inappropriate behavior gets me into trouble. I've noticed that a lot of people accept that the inappropriate advances are just part and parcel of the business and that you can use that element to your advantage. However that always makes me think of a quote I believe is attributed to Sharon Stone, "You can only ever fuck your way to the middle." Shudder at the thought of sleeping with someone to advance my career. I couldn't live with myself! I'm not judging if it's acceptable to anyone else but for me, no can do. I'd rather quit. I mean, of course people end up dating people in the business and it happens that some have a lot of power or are very successful. But that's a whole other conversation. That's life.

I think sometimes my way of being makes certain people uncomfortable and so I just find that it's usually best to just shut my mouth and watch and listen. I remember early on running into situations and I didn't always handle it very gracefully, and I wasn't as aware of the repercussions when you're not careful about how you say things. For example, I was being asked for my opinion, and I actually gave it and I can be a little blunt. Then I remember having this lightning bolt moment: oh…they don't actually want my opinion. They want me to affirm their choice. I realized it was imperative to know when it's the forum to do that, and when it's not. And I think that unless it's your name underneath executive producer, you have to be really careful. It's easy to forget that it's hard for the producers, it's hard for the director, it's hard for all of us to get anywhere in this industry. Your self-esteem can get really beaten up and your ego can be really fragile. And it's important to remember they might be feeling just as stressed and insecure as you, so you send them a little compassion. Don't get me wrong, I don't think it's always this way but you've got to be aware. You can't be a bull in a china shop. You have to have some diplomacy, you have to have some grace, and you've got to know if you're just trying to be right for the sake of being right.

Christina's experiences with the pros and cons in her profession has helped keep her grounded (if feisty) and helped her refine her craft.

Tracey's early experience with "bullshit detection" came with a rather sad example of what happens when adults don't listen to a child's intuition:

Tracey: When I was telling you that story about my principal in public school…it was the strangest thing. When I look back on it now as an adult, standing up and saying, "why, why are you always taking the boys down to the bookroom?" Can you imagine what he thought, looking at me? He thought that I probably knew.

Ville: So he did. I'm sure he was fairly shaken, and with good reason.

Tracey: And then they sent the school psychologist to meet with me, and I was very confused. I'm happy, I have lots of friends, I do well in school,

I was like, what do you guys want? And I realize now that he was trying to find out what I knew!

Ville: Mmm hmmm.

Tracey: And then recently, I went through some issues with my son; the school didn't like some of his comments. He had questions about death and the afterlife, and asked his teacher. They were concerned that he might have some ADD issues, but when I got him tested and he came out fine, they wouldn't accept it!

Ville: Yes, but just try to remember that your son lives his own life and he's got his own mistakes to make. You can't shelter him from everything.

Tracey: No, you can't, but when the school comes to you and says that… it's too much. I talked to a psychiatrist that works for the Canadian government and screens the astronauts for NASA, and he said that there's nothing wrong with him. He said he's gifted, he's high intelligence, and he's just questioning the world! There's nothing wrong with that. So I brought back his comments, and they told me basically that this brilliant doctor didn't know what he was talking about. That was the last straw. I put him into a private school.

Ville: And for a good reason, but you have to understand that they work with so many kids that they have to draw the line somewhere, and if they make an exception, it falls into chaos. That's the same concept that you know, you have to be a shepherd. And as a student, you just have to hope that you get a good shepherd, as opposed to the fellow that you had in your school back in the day.

Tracey: Well, he's in jail now.

Ville: So, there is some good in the world!

Tracey: Actually, all these victims came forward…it took a long time though, this was only about ten years ago. When I opened the paper and saw it, I gasped, oh my God! And just the depth of it too, because he was also working with a few children's charities, there was extortion charges involved, just completely evil. And I realized something very important. Up until finding out about his sordid past, I had always carried the burden of feeling out of place because he had persecuted me so much, and as a child I always wondered if somehow he had been right about me. When I found out about his actual deeds, I was set free. It wasn't me with the problem, it was him.

Ville: Yes, let's just say that that's as close to evil as you can get nowadays. Corrupting something that has not yet bloomed. So, that's weird. I've never been close to anything like that. It just sickens me, but also, there has to be a very sick mind behind it.

Tracey: And it also makes you realize that when something puts your Spidey senses up, or whatever you want to call it, there's usually a reason for it. When something makes you bristle and you're like, wait a minute, what is this? There's usually a reason for you doing that.

Ville: Very true, very true.

∞

The balance point is finding that place where intuition has been measured against personal history. We all have history that makes us more eager to "hear" certain things, and hot button issues that set us off. It's important not to bring your personal baggage to any confrontation so that you can see the truth. This is often easier said than done.

Melissa: I remember a startling example of this when my first marriage ended. I was so sure I understood what went wrong in that relationship and it almost completely fell at my ex's feet. I even psychoanalyzed the guy and pronounced him lacking. I was so sure. So any conversation we had in the wake of that breakup, I had the same tape playing "he's wrong, I'm right, I didn't do anything wrong. It wasn't until a few years later when I was attending a seminar that I realized something pretty key – I was talking crap. The moment of clarity? My wedding vows. We all dwell on the "keep only onto him/her" vow as pretty much the only important one. But there is a whole lot more in the pledge of marriage. There is love, honor and cherish. Yes, I loved in my way but honor, cherish? Not a chance. So there are times when your "bullshit detector" can be on the fritz. The key is recognizing those times.

Alex Grey, photo by Eli Morgan.

Alex Grey is a visionary artist, based in New York City, where his stunning gallery, the Chapel of Sacred Mirrors is located. Known and respected worldwide for the meditative quality of his paintings, Alex has painted the album covers for Tool, The Beastie Boys and Nirvana's In Utero.

Melissa: I had the pleasure of meeting Alex and his family at a seminar in New York during a particularly emotional time in my life. I had just spent a week in the Nevada desert at Burning Man and was processing all kinds of different ideas of who I wanted to be and how to open my mind and heart to be ready for the next phase of my life. Alex's calm, compassionate demeanor was only surpassed by his modesty. When he shared his card at the end of the seminar, I was later surprised to realize I already knew Alex's work and that I had seen it at Burning Man. Coincidence? I don't think so. People present themselves in your life when you need to meet them. I was able to introduce Alex to Rob Brezsny (alternative astrologer, musician) and they found many similarities in their approach to spirituality.

Tracey: Do you think that it is in the nature of a rebel to have a highly developed bullshit detector, as Hemingway suggested? The desire for truth, and the inability to swallow pat answers? Do you feel that this is part of your makeup? How did you channel it to help you in life, as opposed to raging and going off the rails, as so many rebels do?

Alex: Of course, it is important to differentiate between ego and authenticity. That would be my definition of a "bullshit detector." It is not my nature to "rage". It is more in my nature to trust people and take them at face value. Although I do experience inner turmoil, I tend to walk away from conflict. I listen to my inner voices and follow them, hopefully not to my own peril.

We spoke next with our modern day explorer, Bill Jamieson:

Tracey: Do you think that it's the nature of a rebel to have a highly developed bullshit detector?

Bill Jamieson. Photo credit: ©James Ireland 2009, www.jamesireland.ca

Bill: Oh for sure! I have done many jobs that deal with people one on one. From telephone sales, to being a sales representative for a freight forwarding company at the Toronto Airport, to aluminum siding door to door, as well as a general contractor specializing in waterproofing up until I bought the museum. I have always been involved in sales and dealing with people. Within minutes of speaking to someone you know if there will be an opportunity to close a deal or move on. You basically size up the person, and if you feel that there is a chance to do business, you take it. You mirror the person; if he talks about fast cars, you talk about fast cars. It works the same way when I'm buying. Sometimes I'm trying to buy heirlooms that have been in the family for years as I am a collector first, and a dealer second. It is very hard sometimes wearing both hats. In my job, I come across bullshit all the time. The stories I hear in my business today about when artifacts were collected, and when these artifacts left the country of origin are constantly fabricated. There are strict cultural laws in place by countries to prevent smuggling and I have to be very careful that the artifacts I am buying have a pristine provenance. So having a highly sensitive bullshit detector is highly important.

⚇

Neev, the founder of CALM shares his insights on the bullshit detector.

Tracey: Do you think that it's in the nature of a rebel to have a highly developed bullshit detector, and I think of that as the desire for true information and the inability to swallow pat answers. Do you feel that this is a part of your makeup?

Neev: Yes, definitely. If I know enough information, I can do it myself, formulate my own opinions. I was definitely anti-authoritarian. I had a fair amount of blow-back in school because of it. Teachers tried to pawn me off on other teachers. I wouldn't pay attention, and then I would get a B minus and it would drive them crazy. They would always wonder why I wouldn't apply myself because I could get A's and it was because I didn't care. Marks didn't matter to me.

Tracey: So, do you find that is something that's a strong part of what you do now? Be able to see through people and their motivations that aren't necessarily so pure?

Neev: Sure. But I've been at this so long that I think that I live in a bubble. The answer is obvious to me, and yet it's either not obvious or not a high priority to other people. So I live in this bubble and wherever I go, marijuana is legalized, but it's just my own little fantasy world. I live in a special dimension, and it's legal! Almost everybody I know has a medical exemption, it's legal for them, they're knowledgeable, and responsible about cannabis. When I talk to police and politicians, I'm respectful and knowledgeable.

Tracey: But don't you think that we're going to get legalization someday?

Neev: Well, you would think that common sense would prevail. But that seems to be uncommon.

So how does the Successful Rebel find the truth in the every day dealings of our world? A combination of inquisition, self-reflection, self-acknowledgement and compassion for those around them. You don't have to swallow it, you just have to listen. And make your decision based on your gut, your knowledge of yourself and who you want to be; if it doesn't match that, then you can be pretty sure it's BS.

Chapter 3:
Go to Hell, Faust! Not Selling Out

So let's assume you know who you are, you know what you want and doors are beginning to open. How do you know which door to go through? We spoke with Ville Valo about staying as true to your craft as possible.

Tracey: Ville, even though you've sold millions of albums worldwide, the North American public isn't as familiar with you as they should be. It's the same thing my sister has gone through. She's been a lead in many movies and some people still don't know who she is. And then she'll get considered for things that she would never do in a million years.

Ville: Yeah, well, but then again, people like us tend to forget that, for example, Johnny Depp wasn't big before Pirates of the Caribbean.

Tracey: Well, he was big in my mind, but that's a different story, believe me!

Ville: Exactly, and big in anybody else's mind that watches any films. Everybody knew him and thought that he's one of the better actors, and a bit more alternative, in US films. But it's funny how not a lot of average Joes actually knew about him. At all.

Tracey: Yeah, he had to get into a mainstream Disney flick.

Ville: Yeah. And there's nothing wrong with it, but it's so funny because we have enjoyed his films for quite some time, before the mega stardom happened. It's one of those things, you know? You just have to wait for the jackpot. (*As a funny aside, Ville ended up voicing an especially amorous hippo in the Finnish release of Disney's Madagascar 2: Escape to Africa.*)

Tracey: Exactly. Never, never, never give up!

Ville: Well, you know, the aesthetic and tastes keep on changing. And it's not necessarily the wisest decision to create a full picture in people's heads before they have the opportunity to make up their own minds. So it's good to leave them with the opportunity to figure it out for themselves. Nowadays, obviously you have to simplify everything for people to understand everything. As many people understand everything at the same time. But I guess that occasionally spreading like a virus is a better thing.

Tracey: Yes, depending on which virus, right?

Ville: Oh… yeah, well. Well, kind of depending…*laughs* As long as it's not deadly. So it's not too bad. I've just got to be patient because there have been a lot of possibilities for me and for other artists as well to sell their art. And you might have more money for a second, but we don't want to become a brothel. HIM's not a brothel yet. A whorehouse. Or a gigolo house, whatever…

Tracey: Now from what I've read, when you were a kid you were really into KISS, correct?

Ville: Yeah, there were a couple of Finnish bands too at the same time, but I can't really remember. I was just flipping through my old cds and cassettes, and there's KISS and there's Motley Crue, and Iron Maiden and Anthrax and Michael Jackson, strangely enough…

Tracey: The reason I'm asking is that Gene Simmons, he's in business with our billionaire neighbor here in Aurora. They've created an energy drink and a record label that's searching for Canadian talent, and they have big events with gorgeous girls here, just next door to my dealership. It's incredible, and even more so because I was a huge KISS fan as a kid too.

Ville: What? It's an even smaller world. Well, more power to him…

Tracey: What do you think about that type of extreme marketing, in the grand scheme of things? Because I could see as a musician, that's a very fine line.

Ville: Well, I think that Gene's one of the few people that makes collecting money something sexy. Because he's so very brutally honest about it. Because there are a lot of people, especially in the entertainment business that claim that they're in it for the art, only for art's sake, and the emotional depth that they can plunge into, and become whatever, Yoda…or some shit. But Gene, he's always been very straightforward with his stuff, and it still doesn't take the power away from some of their songs. What Gene was always lacking is the emotion, and since he's been more adamant about money, more outspoken, I can really see why this emotion is lacking, if he was only thinking about the dollars, but obviously he does want to write great songs, make as much money as possible, but it does lack the soul of say, someone like Neil Young has.

Tracey: It was interesting that Ville mentioned Neil Young, as he has long been a hero of mine. He truly personifies the Successful Rebel, and his adventures outside of the music industry have been what attracted me to learning more about his career. Neil's son was born with multiple disabilities, and as a way to connect to his son and spend time with him he developed a remote control paddle system for the control of electric trains, got involved with the Lionel Model Train Company and offered this system for sale to the public. His innovations have brought countless hours of joy to children that can finally do what other able bodied kids take for granted; play with toy trains.

Neil Young has been working on alternative fuel cars for a few years, specifically electric engines. He and a team of engineers have perfected the high performance, 100% electric engine and have put it in a '59 Lincoln. They are working out the final bugs, but the vehicle will be ready to roll across the United States sometime within the next year. Neil plans on taking the Linc-Volt as he calls it, on a cross-country trip and film a documentary on the way to Detroit. He has done what I think is the most fantastic thing, and that is bring attention to returning the North American automotive industry to its pioneering roots. He is retro-fitting classic cars, and any other vehicles without having to build new bodies; a stroke of brilliance that I have been trying to do with my Olds 442. Lincvolt.com is his website, if you'd like further information.

Tracey: Has there ever been opportunities offered to you where you stepped back and said no I can't do that, that's just not what I would do? Or felt it was a sell out?

Ville: We don't seem to get a lot of weird offers like that…people know us pretty well, and we're fairly kooky in what we do, and there has to be a spiritual pay off. And it's got to be fascinating on some level…it's gotta be a good story. You know, a million bucks in your bank account does not necessarily equal a good story.

Tracey: And I also think that's more of an American way of doing business.

Ville: It is, and you know, it's a young culture. The North American culture, it's a young culture, and it's based around money, more or less, it's funny how, but good for you, it's based around fancy cars and all that. A lot of materialistic things seem to be very important in surviving, especially socially, in North America. For me, it's fascinating.

Tracey: Yes, but then you end up with people like I'm talking to, people that I want to get the word out to that don't want that, the rebels. Whether or not I sell cars doesn't mean that I think it's awesome to go for the most expensive car, the most flashy car, you know what I mean?

Ville: That's a philosophical debate; you know… why do you get the car? Do you get the car because you like it? Or do you get it because you can afford it, or do you get it because you want to pick up a girl in that car, or, it's like you know, none of those answers are wrong. It's whatever you want to do with it. I don't drive, you know, I don't give a fuck. I'm happy to be in a position to get the bread on the table doing what I love and that's very rare, so basically I haven't had the need to speculate upon how to pay my next rent or my next phone bill for the past maybe seven years. And that's great because I used to steal my toilet paper out of bars and I was counting pennies literally to be able to just concentrate on music, and I wasn't complaining, that was cool at the time, because I knew what I wanted to do and I was happy doing it.

Tracey: But, on the other hand, there's so many mainstream people that walk around with a closed mind, and they judge, and it impacts alternative people very negatively because they don't give the rebels a chance, and they just predetermine what they're going to think about that person, and it cuts off a lot of life's experiences.

Ville: Well… let's say that people like that have pissed me off to such a degree that I really wanted to be more successful in what I did which made me rehearse my instrument, my music more and songwriting and read more to be able to confront those people in conversations about whatever topic, and to floor them. Because I do believe that the pen is mightier than the sword, and just work on your ethics, and bit-by-bit you get there. Nobody is the most intelligent person on earth, or whatever. I just tend to avoid those kinds of people. Hopefully and helpfully, with what we freaks do, we might be able to open up some of those eyes to different possibilities.

Tracey: Well, I think that you've done that with your music. If you look at a lot of the fans that you've got, especially in the States, you have the usual suspects that love Metal, but there are a lot of moms, there are a lot of people that normally wouldn't be into that kind of music. Right? So you have opened up their eyes to something that they normally wouldn't be interested in, which is great!

Ville: Well, it's a combination of so many things, you know? It's been, in my case it seems that people are fascinated about the fact that we are male, yes, and we play the type of music that's normally considered to be fairly macho, and testosterone fueled, and so it is in our case as well, but we are not afraid to embrace our feminine side, or whatever you want to call it, more emotional side.

Tracey: That's true. And the struggle and torment that stems from your emotional side does bring out the artistic expression.

Ville: And it does bring out the best in a lot of people. And it does enhance all the different aspects of that particular personality, good or bad. So it maximizes good or evil.

Tracey: Well, it's like Faust. You've studied that, right?

Ville: Well, I haven't done a deal.

Tracey: *laughs* Faust made that deal with the devil because he wanted that moment of pure happiness, the essence of life. But the reason that he made the deal was because he was so jaded that he believed that it could never come. Otherwise, he wouldn't have made the deal.

Ville: *pauses* It's kind of funny that…it's like there's more than 30 words describing snow in the Eskimo languages, and there's only one word describing love and that's love. And love is always different.

Tracey: What's the Finnish word for love?

Ville: Rakkaus.

Tracey: And there's only one in Finnish as well?

Ville: Yeah. In Latin, I guess they have two different ones; one more spiritual and one more carnal love. But that's about it, and it still doesn't describe everything that a relationship is.

Tracey: You're not into subjugating women, which a lot of Metal is about, and for me, that's what makes you stand out.

Ville: We don't dare to. We know the truth behind you all.

∽

The deals we make in life aren't always in business. Sometimes we sell ourselves out for the dreams and desires of another person, because we seek love and acceptance.

Melissa: This is a huge one for me. One of the biggest regrets I have is returning to Canada after I finished my masters at UCLA. I was coming back to marry my high school sweetheart, but I knew deep in my heart that it was a mistake. It wasn't that I didn't love him; it was that I had sold out who I was in the process. The only way that marriage could have gone was badly, and true to form it did, ending four years later. By then the momentum in my career had passed and a dream of a life in LA was gone.

∽

Christina Cox has tried hard to balance the need to have a paycheck with her personal worldviews.

Tracey: Everyone that gets up in the morning doesn't necessarily put out his or her perfect work every single day. There are times when a singer puts out some clunker notes. It's just the way it is.

Christina: Yes, and sometimes they have to put out a pop song to support the rest of what they do. It's the reality of the job. I think that it's important for me to be responsible in the kinds of things that I will and won't do. There are scripts that my manager won't even let anyone send me, because he knows that I won't do them. There are some things that I just don't want to participate in putting out into the Universe. Horror has come back in a big way. It doesn't cost very much to film, you don't have to have stars in it, and it's universal. There's not too much dialogue. There's screaming and running. And the revenue is huge. And unfortunately, there's so much total and utter violence in movies, TV, the news, that there seems to be this complete desensitization and we've lost the impact of what that kind of violence does. So the horror movies now seem to have to keep pushing the limit, otherwise we don't feel anything. You can't just have a girl getting stabbed, her best friend has to be forced to stab her while they've been kidnapped by a sexual predator in an RV rigged with hidden cameras that transmit to a web address…blah, blah, blah.

Tracey: Well, I can't stand that stuff, and I think that kind of thing leads to desensitization and decadence of society, and puts it into decline, to be honest.

Christina: I think that it's such a complicated thing to say that TV and video games are responsible for all the violence in the world, because they're not. I do think that it's interesting that the ante keeps getting upped. But it's not my place to judge what other people like or watch or what films they're comfortable doing. If you want to do a horror movie, knock yourself out, but it's just not for me.

∞

Daemon Rowanchilde knows all about being offered deals that his rebellious spirit could not accept. He told us a story about growing up and dealing with this.

Self Portrait 2009. Art by Daemon Rowanchilde

Tracey: Was there ever a time in your life when someone in a position of authority offered you a deal, but you declined because you felt in your heart that you would be selling out?

Daemon: Yes. My dad was the first dealmaker. Always. I was the oldest child. I had the most abuse from him, and I got to a point where I was just like, fuck you. And he would say "well, if you come to visit with your other brothers and sisters, I'll do this or that for you." He was one of those types that would bounce back and forth, so he would go on a rampage and I'd build a barricade so he couldn't get at me. I actually did have forts built outside of my window, so I could slip out of the second floor window and hide in them. I had all my escape routes figured out, because it happened all the time. But he would flip out, and he would go on these rampages where I didn't actually know why, there was never a why. It was just, okay, here we go. And then later on there would be this sobbing father leaning over me, looking for sympathy from me. And I wouldn't even talk to him, I wouldn't communicate with him, I would lock myself in my room and he would rebuild the tree fort that I built, as he thought it was better than the way that I had built it. I was unhappy with that, because now it was an adult's concept of my creation. I constantly did not buy into his games, so later on when people tried to make deals with me, I was instantly skeptical because of my upbringing.

Tracey: So there's the double edged sword, right? The torment that you had growing up as a child, but it made you wary, so you didn't get yourself in as much trouble as might have happened as you grew up. Because people are always offering you deals if you're talented, or if you have something to bring to the table; there's always some bastard that wants to buy your ass. One way or another. I've met so many super rich people that have wanted to make a deal with me in one way or another and quite often it's a deal with the devil.

Are you familiar with the story of Faust? Faust was an alchemist in Germany back in the 1640's, and he wanted to experience a pure moment in time that was purely the essence of being human, with joy, the pinnacle experience, the peak experience as a human being. He attracted the devil because he was dealing with alchemy, so the guy's going to have his eye on you anyways, as the spirit world is watching. So the devil comes and offers him a deal and says, "listen, I'll give you what you want, but the moment you get it, your soul is mine". Faust makes the deal, but the only reason that he does is because he was so jaded by that point in his life that he didn't think that it could actually happen. He didn't believe that moment of pure happiness and joy existed, so he made the deal and lo and behold, it did. And the moment it happened, the devil appeared and said "You're mine, baby!"

So have you ever felt like something might have given you momentary pleasure, but you knew that the line had to be drawn? You knew that it would take you down that path to destruction? Because I think it's one of the things that cause a lot of people that are successful, but are on the edge, to go off the rails. Substances, sex addictions, things like that.

Daemon: I believe it's not that moment where you first experience happiness; it's when you try to reproduce it.

Tracey: Ah, that's it, chasing it!

Daemon: When you're not experiencing the real thing, that's when it goes into addiction.

Daemon's wife Raven, agrees:

Raven: Sex and drugs, often the combination of both can become that path to destruction because you're chasing a form of happiness, and not just letting it happen naturally in the course of your life.

Tracey: But the thing with Faust is that because he found that moment in the pure love of a woman, God took pity on him and said "I'll give you a mulligan, and let you out of the deal with the devil, but don't ever do anything like this again." So God overruled the devil, because Faust was redeemed through love. But that's the cleaned up, Lutheran version of the story. The other version has God offering Faust redemption, but Faust refuses it, because to be redeemed meant that he had to leave the devil for good, and lose the power that he was receiving from the dark side. And he wanted that power, no matter the cost. So he comes to a bad end, down into the pits of hell.

Raven: That's because Faust identified with the rebel, and had the rebel nature! He fucked it up, and sabotages! That had to do with his own internal motivation.

Tracey: Yes, and it's a fine line. To use your rebel nature as a tool, but to not be destroyed by it.

Raven: Yes, and it's a metaphor for life. You have a moment when you see everything clearly, everything, your whole path, and your ride on the rollercoaster, and at any time you could have gotten off of that rollercoaster. And God comes to you and says, "whether you get off or stay on that rollercoaster, you're still loved." And at that point people make a choice. They can choose to get off the rollercoaster, or they can lash back and fall back into that self-sabotaging behavior, like falling off the wagon, etc. So Faust is a metaphor for all that.

Tracey: But it's also a metaphor for the questing and questioning in life, because as an alchemist he wanted to know the inner workings of reality, and to turn away from the devil meant that he had to put aside that questioning and just take things on faith. And that was not in his nature.

Raven: And I've seen that behavior in my own life, because when I try to make a change in my life, for health purposes or whatever, my friends that have been around me will laugh and say "sure Raven, whatever", so I'll stay strong for a while, but eventually backslide. And it takes a few attempts for the new behavior to stick, because of those outside forces. I second guessed myself, I got back on the track, instantly realized that I couldn't fool myself any longer, because once again, it's like Plato's Theory of the Caves; once you've seen the light, everything that you've identified as real are really shadows, delusions and you can't go back! And when I finally made the decision, I did it in a very dramatic way, and I literally crushed a substance under my heel and upset one of my friends who said "why didn't you give it to me?" And that wasn't the point. I needed to make a grand gesture to cement the change within myself. But if I backtracked and thought about it, I had this peak experience; I second-guessed it because we are identified in our social sphere as being who we are, so people want us to stay that way. But I finally made the shift and changed. And when you do that, some friends drop off, because you no longer resonate with them. They want to be where they are, and they want you to be there too.

Tracey: I've experienced the same thing, and I find that some of them become very insecure when you make that change. They lash out, or they question your sanity, or they denigrate your decision.

Raven: Or they just drop off. Maybe they come back many years later.

Daemon: Maybe they'll be a friend, but just come back on a more superficial level. A different level. And you just know where your limitations are.

Tracey: I used to feel guilty about that, but now I'm just very blunt that way. When I've had friends that have crossed the line with me, I'm just like "you're dead to me. Don't ever call me again." When somebody has crossed the line where I feel offended, like instances where some have been very rich and they're trying to make some kind of deal with me, like the devil with Faust, I want them to get away from me. Faust made the deal because he didn't believe that his wish could come true, but I know that wishes come true. I know it can happen, and I'm not making that deal, because it will happen.

Raven: But you also need to look at yourself when you become greatly offended, because something about that situation is mirroring your own shadows, and you can learn about yourself greatly from your reaction. Because when you get that strong of an emotional charge, those people are sent to you as teachers. Whether it's to teach yourself about where you need to draw the line to keep yourself authentic, or about your shadow side, you have to listen to it.

Selling out comes in many forms. We sell ourselves out when we deny who we are or what we want out of life. We're sellouts when we accept work or jobs that we know are in direct opposition to what we supposedly stand for. And we sell ourselves out for acceptance all the time.

Ultimately, any act of "selling out" will have the opposite effect — the payoff cannot possibly give us the fulfillment we imagine it will bring, because anything that contradicts our essential nature will not bring happiness – or success.

Chapter 4:
Being in the Flow:
Moments of Joy

"Follow your own star!"

- Dante Alighieri

Is it all hardship? Struggle? Torment? Not at all. There are immeasurable benefits to being the master of your own destiny, of being true to yourself.

Melissa: I remember most of my time at UCLA as being in those moments of divine flow. I was surrounded by people who thought and saw the world in a way I could relate to, who were funny, driven, unique individuals who had given up a lot to be there. And it's not like it was a sensible choice – Screenwriting isn't what I'd call a stable profession. But these were heady days in the mid nineties when six figure spec script sales felt like the norm, rather than the exception. All those nights and days spent at my ancient Macbook cranking out script after script (UCLA had a policy of forcing its writers to produce numerous scripts in rapid succession to get you over hand wringing) was heaven. Music has always been a big part of my process, so the stereo would go on (this was long before MP3 players), the phone would be off the hook and I was literally immersed in my own private movie, currently showing in my head. It was beautiful – and honestly it's the way we should be operating as often as we can.

Ville Valo spoke with us about those moments where you truly are in the "flow" – where ideas come easily and the rewards of your individual pursuit are abundant. Ville is a songwriter, performer and to some degree, the "CEO" of his career.

Tracey: What is the most common path for you from idea to successful manifestation? Do you find that you get a vision of what you want to accomplish or create, or is it more auditory, like do you hear it? How does it manifest for you?

Ville: You mean how a song actually does happen? Well usually, I take a leak and while I'm taking a leak I'm humming. And when I start humming, I hum or whistle something and it's like a paranormal radio type of thing. There are a lot of songs in the air, you just have to know how to pick them out.

Tracey: Right, so you're a psychic radio receiver in a way.

Ville: Yeah, more or less. I guess that it's a combination of me being one of those individuals that can explain my emotions better musically than I can verbally. I guess that the brain's just a sponge that can suck in the information and occasionally I have to let that stuff out, and it's through a song. So when a certain amount of interesting stuff has been going on, you know, I tend to start whistling something new.

Tracey: Okay, that's for a song, but let's say something larger, like a project that you're working on like a new album, or a piece of artwork, do you find that you think about it a lot before it happens, or do you get a clear picture of it and you make it happen?

Ville: Both. It's both. When I was a bit younger, I had a clearer vision of what I wanted to do, but the problem was the actual execution, which I'm better at now. Because on the level of thoughts, and imagination, anything can happen. Then there are the limitations of your hands, your playing capabilities, or your abilities of how to paint. And there are a lot of obstacles, so I tend to come up with an idea and just let it go with the flow. And hopefully, it'll have a domino effect, or a snowball effect with a song. But you can't try to control the project too much before it has happened. Good projects usually, when you tell about a project to somebody, you get information from there. You get new questions from angles that you never thought about, so it's an ongoing process, which is never over.

Tracey: Right. Now, do you find that there are times that you become frustrated because what you have envisioned isn't panning out the way that you would like? Do you find that drives you crazy or does it discourage you?

Ville: At the end of the day, I don't know if I do anything just on my own. I do write the basics of the song and I do get the ideas for song titles and cover artwork and stuff like that on my own, but the fascinating thing about being in this business of music is that you get to meet a lot of creative people and then it's all about not necessarily compromises but trying to understand and value the inspiration behind those people as well. And hopefully having the sum of the parts being a bit more. Rather than trying to do something just on your own, just for the sake of it. Because at the end of the day, anybody who listens to the song or sees the artwork they create it themselves at the same time. With their mind, in how they perceive it.

Tracey: Sure. The way that the other person's brain sees it is their reality.

Ville: Exactly. And through their experiences and what they've been going through in their lives, so it's impossible to really envision something that everyone will see in the same way. Not even a hamburger in McDonald's. It's perceived in different ways by different people, and now we can start talking about consciousness. And the Jung aspect of it and whether there is a greater consciousness, not necessarily God, but is consciousness one big place rather than billions of totally separate places. I can't really say if your red is my red. Maybe yours is wine red and mine is orange.

Tracey: True. I was interviewing a chaneller named Bart Smit and I asked him the question that you posed to him. Do you remember what it was?

Ville: What was the question?

Tracey: It was "what should I do with my life, and why am I not happy?" Do you want to hear what he answered?

Ville: *laughs* Sure.

Tracey: Are you any happier now?

Ville: Well, you know, I'm dancing on the razor's edge. You can see everything in a very unhappy light, or a very happy light. There's a lot of things to be happy about, but also a lot of things to complain about. So depending on your needs, you can be a pessimistic bastard, or a fairly optimistic one.

Tracey: Well, basically he said that your unhappiness comes from the fact that you are a very brilliant individual, but brilliant almost to the point of madness, in that you demand so much of yourself. You walk a fine line and you have to be careful because you always are thinking too far forward, two minutes ahead, three minutes ahead, and you never give yourself a break to relax into the now.

Ville: Yeah, but you can think about the next move in a way that you're thinking about the best possibilities for yourself, to find yourself in a position where you can just let go. So, to prepare yourself, knowing that you might have to, on a mental level, or an artistic level, let's say jump off of a tall building. If you know that in advance, you can put a mattress underneath. So in a way, that does enable you to play around with the possibilities a bit more. It's not necessarily thinking too much ahead. You know, it's kind of like that the main problem usually is that people do get jaded because of substance abuse and all that. Creative people do that because their creativity is based on hypersensitivity. And when you have to work on making yourself as sensitive as possible to all the possible distractions and attractions that the world has to offer, you become easily a hermit in a way, or a watcher. You're just concentrating on so many details, not necessarily doing that on purpose, but because that's the way you've learned your craft. And obviously you get deeper and deeper into it. It's not necessarily a negative thing, but then again, you have to try to combine the mundane with the more extraterrestrial.

Tracey: Do you feel that you're seeing glimmers of happiness at least?

Ville: *pauses* Occasionally. When I'm writing songs, when I'm seeing the crazy way that a song is being born, and how it travels, and takes you around the world, to meet fascinating people, it's a miracle that I asked my cousin "what's a good album to buy" and she said "go with KISS, I love KISS" and I was so young and didn't know shit about music and I just wanted to buy an album. So I bought Animalize by KISS and fell in love with it so much that I decided that I wanted to play and many years after that I was actually playing an instrument myself in clubs, and many years after that I'm sitting here in my old house in Helsinki and I'm talking to you. It's fascinating how far patience and perseverance and going against the grain can take you.

Tracey: So, if you think about now, in your life, what would bring you the greatest happiness? What moments where you feel that pure essence of it? Do you have that?

Ville: *pauses* No. No, and I guess that's the reason I write songs. It makes life more tolerable, I guess. I don't know what I'm looking for. I still haven't found what I'm looking for, Bono Vox once said, or sang. So, I don't know. There are moments of enjoyment. I don't know if moments of joy can be interpreted as happiness. It's like trying to be on the same page when talking about heaven. Or religion, or beliefs, or whatever. I guess tolerance, or a tolerant world would be heaven to me. Then again intolerance does invoke these conversations.

It's clear in conversation with Ville that part of what feeds his creative process is this eternal struggle; the ongoing, everyday decision of "what is happy". For him, being in the flow means embracing the dark and the light and seeing the potential in both.

Let's see what Christina Cox has to say about success and what she calls "your absolute clarity":

Christina: Well, I think that's the upside of a slow and steady career, with success coming as you're ready for it. If you're aware of yourself at all, and it's pretty hard to be aware at 15, you can definitely get yourself into trouble. For me, with all the setbacks it's been easy to stay grounded *laughs*. There have been some years of great success, doing a successful series, shooting great pilots, being on hold for huge films, and then nothing. Then everything will go dry for six month, and you play the waiting game. Then you get something else, and start working again. So it's your responsibility to keep a check on yourself, your behavior and your ego, for your own sake. Your head can get awfully big awfully fast when things are going well. You have to be really careful with what is perception and what is reality and not start believing your own press. That's part of what the machine is doing, it's altering perception in order to sell tickets and it's a necessary element but you can't buy into it. This is not the same thing as playing small; it's being aware and responsible for your life as a whole instead of indulging yourself. Suddenly you're flinging your keys at valets, being rude to the waiter, making ridiculous demands and all that other bullshit. Although I'd wager that personality type was probably doing a variation on that when they weren't famous and I've found that kind of behaviour isn't isolated to performers. Money, success and power can be loaded blessings.

Tracey: Success tends to magnify your true nature one way or another. Now, because success is a process of course, and it's always changing, it seems that part of your makeup wants to be of service. It's just part of your makeup. To talk to other people that have gone through similar problems, especially within your industry, what advice would you give to other people to help them?

Christina: Well, I think that it's always really important to check in with your motivation for doing it. I don't want to come off as negative, but realistic and pragmatic. It's incredibly challenging. Incredibly difficult. So you have to love this. When you're on set, even when you're in class or working on your auditions you have to have the feeling that you are touching your absolute clarity, and that this is what you are supposed to do. If it seems cool, seems kind of fun, big money, you need to give your head a shake, because it's not easy to get there. There are people who I've heard say that it "seems so easy". I once heard someone say, "I was on a set, I watched and it didn't look that hard to me". If it's not your passion, you will suddenly turn around and you will have lost ten years of your life. And you'll say to yourself "what the hell just happened?" It can take so much longer than you think it will. And it can be really hard on your heart. You've really got to love it. Don't take advice from people that aren't working. You can tell the people coming up that are going to make headway, and the ones that will be a background performer with big dreams. There's a willingness to actually hear the advice, the real advice and take it to heart, and it's a really imperceptible difference, but you can tell that they get it. I've been asked, and had friends that have been asked by someone doing background on a show and they're like "so, what's the best way to get a TV series?" And you know that if that's their big question, they don't have a prayer. They're deep in the dream. They're not rooted in reality. If they say something like "I really don't know where to start, or how did you start?" then they have a chance. And once you tell them the truth, the response is very telling as well. Practice, practice, practice. Do as many classes as you can, find out who the good teachers are, be consistent, keep your body and mind in shape, have a life, because you've got to be able to bring your experience to the table. And if they say that their cousin said that they'll take their headshots and they don't think they need classes...uh oh. That's not a great idea, you need training, and you want to have a good head shot. There are some good books about how to get an agent. And then some will say that they've heard that they'll get work if they pay 1500 bucks to someone who'll "represent" them, and you see that not only don't they have a bullshit sensor, they want to hand over their fate to someone else instead of proactively managing their path themselves. You have to be honest and pragmatic, and if it sounds too good to be true, chances are it is. Being young and hot may get you started but you have to be able to back it up. Young and hot are a dime a dozen. Anyone who paints a rosy picture of how easy it's going to be is full of shit. Theatre schools will give you absolutely no information on how to survive in the business, how to get an agent, what makes a good photo, demo reel. They don't tell you to make sure that you have a sideline job that doesn't involve you being in a bar drinking until 2am. Yeah, there's good money to be had bartending and the hours are flexible, but be careful of which one you end up in. What if you have an audition at 9 in the morning, and you don't close the bar until 3am? That's not going to work in your favor. And don't self sabotage by being out partying every night. It's hard work. And you have to be at your best. You also have to not be going crazy because you're not making any money. That being said, and many will disagree but I don't know how great it is to do a ton of extra work, because producers start to know who you are, and they will have a hard time shifting their perception. Because their perception is their reality. And I've worked with some great people who were good actors, but they were identified as a stand in or an extra and it hurt them. It sucks but it's true. It's really hard to do that. You have to have another job, not in the business, while auditioning. Like Harrison Ford with his carpentry. It always helped me to have something else that kept me busy, sane and able to pay my bills. And when it comes to the background thing...I would rather chew my arm off than be on set watching other people do what I want to do. Not to mention you wouldn't be able to get away for auditions. But that's just me. That being said, I have worked with some truly great stand-ins who love what they do, don't want to be actors and are fully present to being great at what they do. It's actually a challenging and important job if you care to do it right.

Christina Cox. Photo credit: ©James Ireland 2009, www.jamesireland.ca

If you do get the opportunity to visit set, then really study how everything is done; learn the process, the etiquette (quietly) so that when you get the job you don't shoot yourself in the foot. Watch and learn, don't just cruise around and eat free donuts every time you get an opportunity to be close to people really doing it, be present, absorb it all or just don't bother. Go do something else, because honestly, this is way harder than it looks. It takes an emotional toll, it takes a toll on your relationships. You'd better be clear that it's exactly what you want to do, and be willing to put in your time to do it right. One thing that they don't teach you in theatre school is how to survive. I learned it by trial and error, because I started getting a lot of work so young. But I made some massive mistakes, politically, and temperament wise, I was not as graceful as I could have been. But you live and learn, and mercifully it didn't hurt me too much.

Tracey: Let's talk about that.

Christina: It happened because I cared so much. And I was so passionate about it but I had no filters and it just didn't come out the right way.

Tracey: Well, I've done that too. We all have, and I think that a large part of it is just a function of youth, to be honest.

Christina: Well, you know, I'm not alluding to things like drinking on set, or doing drugs on set. But having a little impulse control when you're tired or cranky or things aren't going well at home. And more importantly being a professional and not wasting other people's time. Know your lines. Understand what you're talking about. That's your job. Don't learn it in the makeup trailer the day of. On Blood Ties, we'd get guest stars who'd had the script for a week and a half, and they'd show up and didn't know their lines. And then they'd go in their trailer and 5 hours later, still didn't know their lines. And you're like "are you kidding me?" I was stupefied. We have to shoot 12 pages a day. And that's an insane amount of script to shoot in a day. Most shows are shooting 7 pages a day, and on a film, maybe you're shooting four. Or less, if it's a tech heavy one. So on BT, it was imperative to be off book or we wouldn't get the day. We were on such a tight schedule, shooting six-day episodes, when most shows are shooting eight to ten. The rehearsal is not the time for you to learn your lines. You can't be losing takes over people flubbing up their lines. Be prepared. Be respectful. Be respectful of the other people who came to work too. It was a little frustrating, because I was working on three scripts at once, while shooting 14 hrs a day and I knew my lines. You've had it for a week. Why would I want to work with you again? And that's the easy part, that's just the beginning of the work. *laughs* Can you tell this is a pet peeve of mine? ?

Tracey: Did you find that before you got a lot of work that there was any work that you did with visualization, or writing out dreams, or picturing yourself doing that, theatre in the mind, was there anything that you did that way?

Christina: That came later for me, as I became more aware. I started realizing more consciously that I was making some good and some bad choices, certain things made me happy or unhappy. I began asking myself what's making me unhappy? So I started to do some personal work. For me, it's not like I've applied for a job and I don't have the right degree. When you do this and they say "no thanks", it feels like they are actually saying "we don't like YOU". It's really personal, and difficult. And it brings you back to those feelings in school when part of you was hurt that you didn't fit in, that you were an outcast. It can substantiate the belief that I don't belong, that I was "not good enough" and that's why it became so important to do my personal work to get over that and not sabotage myself. Positive visualization is incredibly important because if you can't see it, and see it in a positive way, I don't think that you can have it. I think that if you go in full of fear and needing the job, they smell that need on you like carnivores smell fear on prey. And you will stink yourself out of a job in a few minutes. Generally, if I have an audition for a part that I really like, part of my morning meditation will be to focus on how great it feels to do this job I love without attaching myself to this particular job because if it doesn't happen, I've created expectation and ultimately disappointment. And that energy of expectation is pretty powerful. Expectation can lead to a lot of negative feelings if you don't get what you want, as does entitlement. I find those particularly dangerous areas. I try not to expect a particular job, I just focus on the feeling of being happy, and remember jobs where I was supremely excited about going to set, the feeling of being in the company of people that I enjoyed working with. I think about cast mates that I connected with doing material that I liked. There's a feeling when you drop into your purpose and experience joy. I find that if I can recall images that stimulate those feelings, it's almost like really being there. A film called "What the Bleep Do We Know" gets into this idea deeply and explains how your neurotransmitters really don't know the difference if you're really experiencing it or just recalling it. Think of how toxic that is if you're focusing on the negative! So I think of things that symbolize that feeling of being happy and content on set. On Nikki & Nora, I remember how frigging happy I was to be going to work every day. I see the lights, I see the camera, I see the guy getting the steady cam ready, a street blocked off in New Orleans and getting to film a foot chase through the streets of the French Quarter during Mardi Gras. Does it get any better? The pilot for Nikki and Nora was such a positive experience, I can still remember the song that was playing out of my clock radio at the hotel, and it was Sunrise by Nora Jones. I remember getting up and reminding myself every morning, "This is right. This is the right feeling." And then I'd really enjoy all the little things; that coffee waiting with Liz for the drive into work, being happy to see the crew because you're all rowing the boat in the same direction. And there are no divas, and there's no trouble.

Tracey: Christina has just described the central theme to the self-help classic "Psycho Cybernetics", by Maxwell Maltz. He called it the "Theatre in the Mind". Maltz was a plastic surgeon that discovered that even when he made his patients beautiful on the outside, a lot of them would still be stuck in that negative place. So he created a system to overcome that. For the past several years, I've had a movie running in my "Theatre in the Mind": it was a scene of me speaking to a large group of people in front of Parkwood, the palatial estate and mansion that belonged to Colonel Sam McLaughlin, the founder of McLaughlin Buick and General Motors in Canada. Colonel Sam has always been a personal hero of mine, as he invented the fifth wheel, which was a revolutionary invention in the automotive industry. It was the first turning mechanism which allowed the front wheels to turn independently from the chassis, and it propelled the McLaughlin Carriage Works to become the largest carriage company in the British Empire, with yearly sales of over one million dollars. That was a lot of money back in 1908! Colonel Sam was also the CEO of Famous Players

Theatres, and invested heavily in the burgeoning movie business. As a child in Oshawa I toured the estate on a school field trip and was intrigued by his success and forward thinking. Even back then, I felt a need to study successful people. So in my "Theatre in the Mind", I saw myself speaking in front of a large group of people at Parkwood, telling people about Colonel Sam's legacy and motivating them to once again embrace the pioneering spirit of the emerging automotive industry. I've played this personal vision over and over in my head, because I have strong feelings about it.

I feel that in North America we have forgotten about what has made our countries great, and have slid into a lazy attitude of entitlement. I know that we can regain our edge, but we need to be reminded of the way that we became world leaders and innovators in the automotive industry, and that was through hard work and thinking outside of the box. Rebels and pioneers made the automotive industry great, and I hope that one day we will rise again. I see glimmers of it in the custom and classic car industry, so I am hopeful.

An interesting thing happened this summer. My family went to Parkwood for McLaughlin Day celebrations, and as we walked up to the front of the estate, a news team was there looking for someone to interview. The reporter approached me and asked if I would do an interview about the meaning of McLaughlin Day. So there I was, speaking in front of a large group of people about Col. Sam's legacy, in front of Parkwood. Just like in my personal movie that I had running in my mind. Not exactly how I pictured it, but very close. And who knows what the future will bring?

Our conversation with Christina left us with another perspective on "being in the flow" – there is a certain amount of work that needs to happen before, during and after to not only find it, but also use it to its greatest advantage. The resounding note of her interview was this: if you're not feeling that moment of clarity, beauty and resonance, then you're probably in the wrong place.

Daemon Rowanchilde and his wife Raven use the "creative flow" in their work all the time. Dreams, symbols, and the interpretation of seemingly random events play heavily in their process.

Tracey: So Daemon, tell me what your dream was last night.

Daemon: Well, it doesn't really make sense in normal reality, but on one level I was tattooing these digits...zero, zero, zero, etc...eight zeros and a one...it was a certain precise measurement...over and over again, and it was in my whole sleep, and it was on skin, not on any specific individual...it was like Cosmic tattooing. And somehow my precision was an obsession...I was obsessing over it. It was a code for something.

Tracey: Maybe the code to the secret of life?

Daemon: Could be. Or the secret of waking up to get out of the dream.

Tracey: Was it a disturbing feeling?

Daemon: No, it was just like I had a sense that I needed to wake up out of this dream and stop stressing over it. This precision thing, just so I could sleep better.

Tracey: Maybe it was just your subconscious trying to figure out how to do this sigil tattoo, since it's a new thing for me [a sigil tattoo is a symbolic talisman that bears significance to the wearer – but may be entirely "meaningless" to an outside observer].

Daemon: That's what I think it was. It was just doing it in some bizarre way. But on another level, I think that I was figuring out the tattoo, and on a cosmic level, maybe it was manifesting. That's the only thing that feels right; that I was sorting it out on another dimension, on a different level, and it manifested as your tattoo. Because on some level of reality, your tattoo is already there. And it's important to remember that a tattoo is never just a tattoo. It is always more, no matter what some other tattoo artists might like to say. It can greatly facilitate healing, and healing always happens in the moment, not in the past or the future.

The secret to finding the flow, for each of these individuals was finding what was uniquely interesting to them, and which they were suited to. It didn't matter that they were rock stars, tattoo artists, actors or essentially Indiana Jones, it didn't matter that these aren't considered "wise" career choices. It is who they are – it gave them joy, even if fleeting and it had a sense of being "right". Until you can find those moments where time passes without notice, where you have a sense of being connected with the divine, you are not in the flow.

Keep looking. It's the only true path to success. Most importantly, it's what we're here for.

PART 2

Chapter 5:
Dulling the Monkey Brain

"If you hate your parents, the man, or the establishment, don't show them up by getting wasted and wrapping your car around a tree. If you really want to rebel against your parents, out earn them, outlive them, and know more than they do."

- Henry Rollins

Living authentically isn't always easy. Living with a form of artistic genius that comes often, sporadically, or at inopportune moments can be tremendously taxing. The hours of those in alternative professions can often be grueling and erratic – spend 18 hours on a movie set for an example of the glamour of being an actor.

Sometimes it's just the level of mental activity that causes the trauma. How does one dull the overly active cerebrum? Unfortunately many "afflicted" individuals will turn to drugs and alcohol to quiet the "monkey brain"- what Buddhists describe as the "endless chatter" of the disquieted mind.

Everyone we spoke with had experienced times in their life where this propensity for the brain to idle on long after the task at hand was completed was a serious problem. They solved this with various forms of self-medication, meditation and sometimes just simple acceptance that "there goes my brain again".

One of the people we spoke to who experienced a very public challenge while quieting the "monkey brain" was Ville Valo.

Tracey: So you're saying that you ended up in rehab because of the fact that it was just the time, or that your health was just so impacted?

Ville: Actually, it was just because I had been partying for ten years straight. *laughing*

Tracey: Yeah, that's rough... *both laugh*

Ville: I was just trying to calm my nerves down…self-medication, you know. That's how being in a band starts. You play your first gig, at least here, they happen on the weekends, and the first gig is a celebration, and then you get a bigger gig in a bigger club and you celebrate…you know, it's just a big pile of parties. That's how it is, and you end up being paid in beer. And obviously, you tend to enjoy going out, and the more you do it, it just wears you out.

Tracey: Well, aren't you coming up to an anniversary of not drinking?

Ville: Uh, yeah, next Saturday it'll be a year…

Tracey: Well, congratulations...

Ville: Well…I'm not done yet. You never know, I might be off into a bar…

Tracey: It's funny, because I read quite a bit about you going through that, because my husband quit drinking over two years ago now. He was a chef.

Ville: Oh God, a chef, you don't even have to tell me how they are… people think that being a musician is the worst, but people in sports, athletes and chefs, and doctors, the pressure is enormous, and many turn to drink.

Tracey: Yes, I heard some stories about doctors…drunken doctors delivering babies.

Ville: Yeah, that has occurred, and I'm fairly certain that it didn't happen when I was born, but maybe I was dropped or something and that's the reason that I do what I do... *laughs* No, but doctors have the access to everything, and you know...it's like they're in a constant one on one AA meeting all the time; hear people whine about their problems... emotional problems.

Tracey: It's tough.

Ville: Yeah, it's fucked up, being a doctor, listening to people whine, and having all that access to medication, you start self medicating...

Tracey: Well, with my husband, he was a chef for a few billionaires; their demands can be insane.

Ville: I know, but it's a tough business, being a chef...if you are in really big places like London or New York, and you have to do six day weeks, sixteen hours a day, no wonder you do a lot of blow, and you do a lot of speed, and then you have to calm yourself down with a zillion drinks, so at the end of the day, if you really think about it, all jobs that you really do care for and you're passionate about, all possible jobs are really stressful and you have to find the balance and a lot of people find the balance, not necessarily when it's too late, but when it's on the verge of being too late.

Tracey: I agree.

Ville: William Blake said you never know what's enough, unless you know what's more than enough.

Tracey: That's true. But it got to the point with my husband where I physically abused him. He came home drunk, and it was the last time. I felt terrible after, but I had reached the breaking point.

Ville: My God.

Tracey: And I told him, it was either the drink, or me. Choose now. And that was it, it was done. He quit drinking, and has never touched it since.

Ville: Well, you know...it's never that simple.

Tracey: Well, of course...then you have to work out the reasons why you're doing it. And he actually stopped being a chef, is what happened. Because of that stress.

Ville: Fair enough, yeah.

Tracey: And I think that a sober man doesn't tend to elicit such strong reactions from women…I find drunken men infuriating. Are there any positive things that you've seen from not drinking? Physically?

Ville: The only physical thing is that I've lost a lot of weight.

Tracey: My husband saw the same thing, he's slim now, very, very slim.

Ville: Same happened with me. The excess fat just came off. The bloatedness.

Tracey: The bloat! *laughing*

Ville: Yes, the bloat! The love bloat! But, you know…it was fun while it lasted. I'm not complaining, it could have been a lot worse. You know, I was stupid enough to get myself in such a state, but then I was wise enough to get over it. For now. I don't know what's behind the corner. I'm not stressing about it. I'm not in AA or anything. I just want to make my parents proud and I want to behave myself. We've gone through a lot of shit, everybody has, and I don't feel comfortable with the idea of spending all my free time in a bar getting fucked up. But I got a lot out of it. I got great friends that I still hang out with. I just order a coffee. I met a lot of beautiful ladies, I heard a lot of beautiful and ugly stories, I was able to incorporate in songwriting and I saw the nightlife of the world, which is great. I'm really thankful that I was a fuck up, and now it's time for me to see the day side of the world.

Tracey: I understand what you're saying. For me, I can't physically handle more than a couple drinks, but I go out with my friends for the comradery, not to get drunk. Or was it about the getting drunk for you?

Ville: I don't know. For me, I guess it's both. You cross a certain threshold into full-blown idiotism. It's a combination of all those things. And at the end of the day, I wouldn't be here talking to you if I hadn't done those things. I've met a lot of people and I've made a lot of career decisions because of great, debauched nights out with certain people, so it's all pieces of the same puzzle. We're maybe just describing a more shady area in that beautiful landscape type of picture.

Tracey: *laughing* That's right, maybe just the darker area of the picture.

Ville: Yeah, you know, maybe the shade under Santa Claus's beard!

Tracey: I know what you're saying. You have your wild times when you're younger, which I did, and now, other than the fact that I've got different tattoos that I'm having done and working on, yeah, my parents are proud of me. I do what I do, and I don't do anything that they don't like.

Ville: Well, yeah, but again, we might quote Blake that the road of excess eventually leads to wisdom. You aren't able to know the maximum amount of partying if you haven't crossed it. And that happens with everything. You have to test the limits and I have, and there's a lot more limits I can test, and see how far I can take those things. Being fairly eccentric, just coming back to the topic, I just think that it's a lonely road. More or less. And there are no rules, and that's the beauty of it, because you make the rules as you go. With your freakness. Your royal freakness.

Tracey: So, you didn't go to AA when you were trying to stop drinking?

Ville: Well, AA…if it helps a person to get through a really rough day, but I didn't use it.

Tracey: It didn't resonate with you?

Ville: Well, AA is an addiction itself, isn't it? It's a congregation for people that need a crutch, to bellyache or whatever kind of ache. I get a fucking existential headache out of it.

Tracey: From what I read, it was almost bringing out the rebel in you, having to deal with it in rehab, right? Because of the having to pray to God, and that God is the only one that can help me out in this, and all that kind of stuff…

Ville: Yeah, in that sense I wanted to prove that me being a musician, I didn't throw my drink away from my home, I work in bars, I hang out in bars, I know a lot of people that are fucked up, my friends drink...so I think that in some ways it's a way to switch one addiction for another... or method of coping with the world for another. But whatever works for each person. I've seen it work miracles on some people who are really bad. It was socially giving them something that they weren't able to allow themselves to open up in their ordinary circumstances, so that was their safe haven to admit their problems without being judged.

Tracey: Almost like a therapist.

Ville: Almost like a religion. Like saying your hail Mary's, and then you're fine sleeping with that underage girl, if you know what I'm saying. And you can always dig dirt. People way too easily shovel dirt underneath their carpets. So it's always good to clean it out. Dirt's not good, and I'm allergic. I don't have carpets.

Tracey: You don't have carpets? It's all hardwood?

Ville: Yeah, so that may be one of the reasons for my insanity.

Tracey: Have you still stopped drinking?

Ville: Still stopping! I haven't started again, let's put it that way. The best reason for my recovery being successful so far has been the fact that I haven't had a plan of not drinking. I mean with drinking, there's always that little devil on one shoulder and angel on the other. People are always more interested in the forbidden fruit, and if you deny yourself the possibility of doing something then you want to do it, more and more! At least subliminally, and it ends up being a situation where you tear yourself apart by trying to do both. You can't, so I don't want to restrict myself.

Tracey: Of course. But you and I were talking about the fact that once you stopped drinking, then everybody was like "oh, well, it was such a waste of time" and you were saying that no, at times that kind of thing can be productive! It's not necessarily that it's a hundred percent evil to drink.

Ville: No, of course. Good times, good times. I sucked in a lot of information, I met a lot of interesting people that were necessary career wise but then again necessary in writing all the songs. Without meeting all the people and seeing all the things I did from different perspectives through being fucked up or whatever, I wouldn't be here.

Tracey: I understand your point, but it can be difficult, because you get puritanical people saying that drinking is evil and you'll never get anywhere, and then when you talk to people and see the amazing things that altered states lead to, you see that it's not always bad. But how do you say that without people completely demonizing you?

Ville: I guess that a lot of the people that try to demonize you because of that, they do their 9 to 5 thing. And if you have to be able to do physical work from 9 to 5, 5 days a week, it is a different world. But then again, I think that in the situation that we put ourselves in, bit by bit, being an artist of sorts, I guess the substances and such, it's about letting your guard down. So it's basically, chemically trying to get into a point where you're more of a kid, and when you're able to see the world with a bit bluer eyes.

Tracey: So, not so jaded and not so judgmental.

Ville: Yeah, and not through the history that was taught us in school. But rather in a very empirical fashion, trying to explain it to yourself, by yourself. Rather than believe what you read.

Tracey: Right. So, for you, the fact that at this point you've given up drinking, do you have an outlet for partying?

Ville: I don't do anything.

Tracey: Do you miss it?

Ville: Ah…yeah.

Tracey: I bet.

Ville: Occasionally, I just miss the total lack of control. That's the only thing I miss. But I don't miss feeling ill, I don't miss fucking up my relationships, I don't miss the bad gigs, so there were a lot of negative aspects. It's more about the transcendental getting fucked up. The laws of the universe won't touch me for the next hour. I'm not talking about drug-induced megalomania. It's just about letting go. And that's kind of the toughest thing about getting sober is the way that I get so introverted. Playing a lot of music and all that, but my social life is nil.

Tracey: Sure, because if you can't go out and party with people, you probably feel left out, to be honest.

Ville: Yeah, for sure, but there's a time for everything. And you know, considering that the better part of the past ten years was spent in bars, it's not necessarily a negative thing to be a hermit. And play a bit more acoustic guitar back home. I guess that there's a balance between those things, and I just have to wing it. I don't want to think about it now too much. But for me it was always the booze. Through that you meet so many interesting characters. It's something that does bring a lot of cultures together. The drink after work, or going out and crying into your pint of beer, it's just a very common thing to do. And you know, I was a big fan of Barfly, the movie, and Bukowski as a writer. So obviously it was interesting for a bit to see how low you can go.

Tracey: Yes, and that's another reason that I sent you that Alex Grey book. He speaks about that. It is a large part of an artist's experience to hit that bottom for the artistic torment that some need to create. A lot of the time, through the ages it is something that artists have done. Whether or not it's self-induced, or they put themselves into situations to cause it, that kind of phoenix rising from the ashes, it's a necessary part of the artistic temperament.

Ville: Well, but I guess that most of the time it's just wasting time. It's more like a shamanistic thing; you can induce that with pain or whatever. It's just a way of getting out of this everyday world for a bit. The torment part of it, I guess that it's more about trying to search for your limits. See how far you can take it. See the world from as many angles as possible. And because when you are happy and content, it doesn't necessarily take away the urge to create. To create, you don't have to be in a shitty position. It's just that artists are generally very moody persons, probably because of their sensitivity and since they are reckless at times as well. They tend to abuse the sensitivity and abuse themselves, because they don't know what to do with themselves. They feel like a bit of an outsider. And don't we all. And people tend to medicate themselves differently.

For Ville, drinking brought both good and bad. Although he can't continue on the same path, he does recognize that a certain amount of that "overindulgence" was part of his development.

∞

Sloan Bella

In contrast, Sloan Bella found that substance use actually increased the level of activity in her brain, to an uncomfortable level.

Tracey: So basically, you were dealing with the spirit world contacting you from an early age, but that's the reason that you have the success that you have, because you have that ability. It's just the learning how to control it, is that correct?

Sloan: Yes, it's learning how to control it at that age, but then at my age now, it's about learning how to open it back up to where it was when I was a teenager. When I was a teenager I was far more open in such a brilliant way, a really outstanding way, but it was hard to live. See, you're not going to be sober; you're not going to be living a normal life. I had a very hard time living a normal life. In order to live a normal life you do shut elements of that down. You can't be out of reality and in reality at the same time.

Tracey: So did you find that you shut it down through drinking or medicating or that kind of stuff?

Sloan: For me shutting it down was more a matter of being sober. If I drank or did drugs it would open me up so totally that it was paranoia invoking. I also found that (and this may sound really strange) that certain geographic locations are far more overwhelming for me. Anywhere closer to the east coast, and even if I have to go to New York, I'm far more open all of the time. It's exhausting. It is too much. Every time I go back to do Montel's show, I can't shut it off. I will stand in the hotel lobby and give messages from spirit to strangers. I step foot on the east coast and that's what happens. I go west and it softens up for me. It comes in a different way. On the east coast, it's very physically energetic with my body, so it's much harder to deal with. And people don't live that way, so you run into a lot of people looking at you like you're crazy. They think that it's weird that you're doing what you're doing, or seeing what you're seeing. Many times as a teenager, I would see things and I would just blurt it out, and many times it would be about someone close to them that was going to die. I didn't know how to edit these things, and it was very strong, and people don't want to hear that. It was very difficult in that sense. I would see everything out of body, so as a teenager, if somebody died, and many of my friends did die, I would see it. Car accidents, motorcycle accidents and idiotic behavior. When they would die, I had an issue with narcolepsy, almost in the sense that my body would shut down and I would sleep in a corner somewhere. Any corner, anywhere, on a street, on a bus, it didn't matter. I would step outside of my physical body and see the people and be able to communicate with them. I was constantly doing that, like every twenty minutes passing out for a few seconds and then waking up. That was continuous. I've not done that since I came west, thank God. I've researched why it happens with me geographically, and it seems that it's your birth energy. You come in with a chart in a certain area, and that was my gift in that area. When you move, the chart changes. It's like you move into a different climate, but it's a different spiritual energy climate. You relocate the chart and it becomes a different energy. It's expressed in a different way. It makes the chart almost as if you're born in the west, because that's where you are staying physically.

Tracey: So, maybe for people that are having a hard time with success and keep running up against obstacles, maybe if they just changed their geography or location they would find it to be beneficial?

Sloan: Absolutely. It could be much easier somewhere else. It removes blocks, or it brings in blocks, depending on where you are. When I came west, it changed my chart. When I go back I become my birth energy, which is extremely intuitive. I remember seeing spirits around my bed all the time. Try telling your parents that when you're a young child! After the fifth time, they're telling you that you're crazy. They think that you're making up things for attention, or you're lying. Whatever it is, so that they can explain away what's going on. It's difficult. And when you come from an educated household, with people who have degrees, and education and logic it's very difficult.

∞

Melissa: In very "unwriterly" fashion, I didn't turn to alcohol to stop the constant thread of thoughts, ideas and responsibilities. A writer truly is never "finished" or "off duty"- ideas continuously swirl and nag to be written. While working on one project, you're thinking of the ten others that are being ignored. My drug of choice? Food. Sadly, a skinny writer with a drinking problem seems much more interesting than a "Rubenesque" writer with the same talent! I struggle with this particular "monkey" to this day.

Will a truly creative, rebellious individual ever quiet the "monkey brain"? We're not sure you'd want to – for while this incessant chatter can create chaos, it is also the creative force. The key remains finding the balance between creativity and madness, between control and the loss of control. We're working on it. And that's all you can ask of yourself.

Chapter 6:
Pain and Suffering:
What Doesn't Kill Us...

"It makes you feel good to know that there's other people afflicted like you"

- Harvey Pekar

Choosing any career is no guarantee of success, or of security, but choosing a career in an alternative profession may seem especially daunting.

Consider this: there has never been a better time to choose the profession that you feel is your personal calling. Why, you ask, in this climate of complete uncertainty would anyone want to go out on a limb? Because there is no limb to go out on! There is no such thing as guaranteed success, of a "right" path to success in our current economy. So why not take the risk on something that means something to you, rather than selling out for an MBA that no one will want?

We spoke with Christina Cox, an actor who understands better than many how long and hard the struggle is to build a career and make a living.

Christina: The major pool of talent is really small and it's really hard to break into. And as a woman especially, you're up against names of people who have 15 studio features to their credit. I went to see Wanted, and I was talking about it to a male actor friend of mine, and he was disappointed that he hadn't even gotten to read for any roles in the film. Not even Thug Number 4. And I was like "dude, how many women were in that film?" And how many women over 32? One woman! For a feature that probably had 40 guys in it.

Tracey: So the playing field has even narrowed down to that point.

Christina: Yeah. And the way that they've budgeted the films, and the way that it in turn affects the way that they're written. When I started out, there would be 3 million and under independent or straight to video, and then there was a 10 million dollar independent that would do the festival circuit, and then there was a bunch of studio movies between 22 to 50 million dollars, where it was going to be a good looking film, it had a decent cast, you maybe got to go on location somewhere cool, and there would be more than three characters in it. There would be some leads, there would be some decent supporting but those movies are gone. That mid budget studio feature is almost non-existent.

Tracey: What is that a function of? Why do you feel that's happened?

Christina: Everything is going into the Spiderman. The Ironman. Hellboy. Giant blockbusters that are costing 250 million dollars. Which when they're good, I enjoy as much as the next person. But how much money do you think is left over for little movies? They're pooling all the money into what they hope will be massive opening weekend revenue, and it's not leaving a lot of cushion in the budget for smaller films. And because those films have so much riding on them, they're going to load that cast with box office names. Bankable names.

∞

Sloan Bella has had more experiences with those that check out of this lifetime at their own hands, whether by accident or with purpose. Pain and suffering don't end with the end of life, as Sloan found out on numerous occasions.

Tracey: What about those people that kill themselves, are they messing with that predestined time?

Sloan: Yes, they are messing with their path and changing everyone's path that surrounds them as well. I think that I have first hand knowledge of that. Here's an interesting thing that I wanted to say. You know when people say things like pornography is a victimless crime, hard drugs are a victimless crime, and you know, as a teenage person I would have agreed with that. But it wasn't until I lived through my teenage drug years, and I'm still alive and talking to you. It wasn't until I married my husband, and his son was 11 months younger than me. He had children from a first marriage. When I met the son and watched him go through his drug addiction, my karma slapped me right in the face. Because, I lived through it, but the havoc it caused while my parents assumed that I was going to live or die, or whatever, I actually watched my stepson die from that. He died of an overdose, and our lives have never been the same since. Even though I knew it was going to happen, five years before the accident I saw it. I would see visions of it. Karma, I learned at that time, I lived it in my own life, but then I lived it as a parent figure to this person. I watched it happen and it totally corrupted our life. Our lives went in a completely different path, my children have suffered from it, my husband has suffered from it. The grief and the horrific situations; our lives have been altered so incredibly. I can't even describe how much it changed everything. The interesting thing was that intuitively I saw it happening. I gave birth to my son and I was twenty-nine, and then I saw my stepson dying in a vision. I actually told his girlfriend in a reading, as a warning, that he was going to die if he didn't get help. And then I said to my husband, we are going into a five year period in our lives where I see only grey. It's like grey San Francisco airport fog. I can't see out the other side and I have no idea what's happening. I can't feel or see anything in that. My husband refers to the first five years after that happening as complete and utter hell. But spirit would not show me anything. I gathered by the feel of it that it was my karma. And I realized through the situation that drug use and addiction is not a victimless crime. Other people get hurt. The people that are left behind suffer and even though I try to think that it doesn't affect me, if affects me in every choice that I make in parenting my children. I overreact. If I even think that they're doing anything like that, I become like an insane person. I just won't have it happen. But being given that information by spirit, and then finding that you can't stop it is also perplexing. What's the point of that? You can't prepare for that. I thought that I was, but I truly wasn't. So to see it as a vision, what is the usefulness of it?

Tracey: Maybe the way that your psychic ability expresses itself is that you're like a radio receiver, and you never know what song is going to be played on it. You never know what you're going to pick up.

Sloan: Right. You don't know. In my development, my best friend died when I was seventeen. He was on a motorcycle and some idiot turned into him. It was weird, because when he died no one had told me because I was unreachable, and I had searched for him the day he died. And then he came to me that afternoon after he had just crossed over and showed me what it was like for him. He basically set me on my path. He cemented my career at that time. So I was very lucky to have my career cemented at such an early age.

Tracey: He came to you, and what did he actually say?

Sloan: He told me that I would be okay. Which was important, because I was an insane teenager at the time. He showed me that light and said "this is your path". He put me on my path in his death, from the other side. I tried to get away from it. I've owned restaurants, I've owned bars, I've become a hermit, a gym rat, I've become all of those things, and yet people find me. It's truly my path, so I'm actually blessed with that. Many people do not know what they're here to do. I do know.

∞

Raven Rowanchilde's early experience with religion brought her a new perspective on pain and suffering – was it really necessary?

Raven: I was seven years old and it was in church. I looked at the suffering Christ on the cross and there it was. You have to suffer through this life and then you die. What was the point of it all? We glorified these icons of suffering and martyrdom, and I just felt that by focusing on all the suffering, we were attracting more of the same. I don't think that I had formed this complete train of thought, but it definitely began at that moment in Church, and it sent me down the path that I'm on today.

Daemon: For me, that kind of thinking was more fully developed in my early teens. There were different stages. Those levels of realization were earlier, but I wasn't fully aware. I developed parts of that kind of awareness.

Tracey: Was there a specific moment where you lost your innocence and said to yourself "now I know the way things work." That feeling, that shift?

Daemon: I think it was with my father. I think it was when I finally stopped playing the game of trying to make him the perfect father, and trying to figure out what was wrong with me. I realized, holy fuck… at that time…he's a fucking asshole! I could actually accept that idea that an adult was not superior to me, just because they were an adult. And of course that reflected on all reality, because before that I thought that all adults were better than me as a child. After that I thought that adults were fucking idiots.

Tracey: And it's especially distressing when it's your own father who's a figure that you want to have as your hero, basically.

Daemon: Exactly. You have to let go of that dream. Now I realize that that was all a gift. Because it made me have to think, and not accept the status quo.

Tracey: You began to search for the answers instead of look to them, the middle of the road, minivan majority way that life is supposed to be. That's why you have so many problems in the public school system, because the parents and teachers are not fulfilling either their or their children's lives, honoring the gifts that those kids were brought into the world with.

Daemon: I think my moment of realization was when my father's second wife, (and he had many), came to visit us. We were pretty friendly with her, even though she was really screwed up…I think from being with him. Anyways, she took a cab from Montreal to Ottawa and came without any word of warning, just showed up at the door, with a cab driver waiting in the car. She had no money, but she had champagne… she was an alcoholic, and she had champagne and took me into the back room, supposedly to help me open the bottle of champagne.

And my friends ran into the backyard, and they're all making faces at me trying to make me laugh, while she's trying to tell me this very serious story while she's quite drunk. While I'm trying to open the bottle, she's hiking up her skirt and going here let me help you…and at the same time she's telling me that she's pregnant with my father's child and it's going to be twins and they're going to be blonde haired and blue eyed, identical twins and she's going to die at their birth and I've got to take them into my custody. Now, she was Grenadian, so the dark skin and brown eyes, and my father had dark hair … anyways, she's telling me this, and my friends are trying to make me laugh though the window…I realized that I have to be the understanding adult here… they're the fucked up children. At that moment, whoosh!! Everything changed. I wasn't angry. Anger before had clouded my judgment. I wasn't angry, I just saw the whole picture and I said okay. This is how things actually are.

Tracey: Yes. It's like the Emperor has no clothes. They've been running our show and they can't even drive. Why am I putting up with this? And for some people, it's not just one situation. It's a steady drip. But I think that most successful people that are outside the norm they have that growing awareness of reality, but it's how you train yourself to channel that energy, because the problem is if you just rage at things, your life just falls apart. You have to temper it. You have to use the tools of the establishment. Because sometimes it's not anger, it's just passion, and there's so much energy behind it that people become offended. You have to control it, and channel it.

Daemon: Yes, or else you burn yourself up. Burn out, and burn out everybody around you. You need to learn how to channel that passion and use it for your own ends.

Tracey: You could be the smartest person in the world, but if you can't get people to listen to you, you can't get anything done. You need buy in, you need people to want to listen to you.

Daemon: I wonder sometimes with the frustrations of an artist, or a creative person feels when other people see them as successful… they've reached a certain stage of success, but they're not happy. I've been there. I think that it's a part of yourself that knows that you're not reaching your true potential. According to other people, they think that you've reached the top, and some part of you intuitively, inside, like maybe the outside part of you is believing the status quo and is going "whoa, I'm successful", and you are to a certain degree, but some part inside of you, your wisdom is saying "you haven't even attained a fraction of your true potential." And you can't figure out how to break past that next part that's holding you back. And that's really depressing, frustrating, everything, because you've hit what you thought was your potential, and then you feel that something's not right.

Tracey: And I think that's why a lot of successful people, artists, whatever, self-destruct and self-medicate too. There's a lot of that that goes on, and that is its own path to destruction.

Daemon: And self-medicating is trying to suppress the part of you that has bought in to the mainstream (even though you're a rebel), a large part of you is not really the rebel, and is buying into the system! And you're trying to figure out "what part of me is buying into the system?" The rebel part of you is self-medicating, because you can't deal with it. Whereas you need that sensitivity, that suffering, that pain to clear the parts off that will then reveal the new you and your new potential that you held back from. The self-medication just holds you where you don't want to be. Maybe Jimi Hendrix or Janis Joplin, those people that died through self medication, they died where people thought was the pinnacle of their careers, but who knows what would have happened if they didn't self destruct? What if they had broken out of that and reached a whole new level? For someone else that was mind blowing, what they reached, but maybe that was not even a fraction of what they could have done. So maybe a lot of artists hit that stage of being alcoholics, or drug addicts, or just depressed or whatever, maybe it's because they just haven't figured out how to break out. They're still holding on to some belief about society, and if they could just let go of that belief.

Tracey: Well, I think that's why somebody like a Neil Young got to the top of the game with his music, why he continues to do different projects, like electric cars and the environment, custom cars, why he's got businesses that way and I think that's why super achieving rebels have to keep their minds occupied and they always have to be going towards a bigger and better goal. Or a different goal.

Daemon: Like you were saying earlier about the process being the important thing, not the goal. That alchemical process, you see the surface of it, like customized cars or whatever, all these different creative projects, so you see the surface but there's something else going on underneath all that, like a deeper process and undercurrent. Say you're really good at music, and you're a musician and you're successful...if you only pursue that because it's the strongest part of your creativity, if you only pursue that and you don't pursue other creative projects, you could be missing some little ingredient in your own personal process and that's why you feel lost. Ken Wilber, one of the foremost philosophers of our time says that the integral approach where you don't just pursue one thing...it's like cross training; you don't just strengthen one muscle in the arm and let the others atrophy, so that one muscle could be your music thing or your painting, or whatever. So you strengthen that one, but you still have to be aware of all the other organs and muscles in the body. And the energetic levels and every other dimension and balance it all out, so you have to integrate it all, you can't just, based on society reacting to your musical talent, you can't just do that. Even though you're considered a success, you might get wasted all the time, you might have difficulties with relationships, or whatever. You have to work on those things too, for true success and happiness. Wilber says you can have a Buddhist monk who is fully realized on one level and can zip into exalted states at will, but maybe he's a misogynist or a homophobe. There are different lines of development, and one can be really developed and the other can be fucked up. So if you buy into other people's belief systems, so you think you're a rebel, and you are on one level but then there's another part of you that completely bends and conforms, that's where the self medicating or depression comes in, because you're trying to suppress that knowledge. You can express your true self on some level, but you're letting everything else go to hell, because you're still buying in to the norm on another level. The danger of a preconceived notion of being a rebel or being a freak can go against you, because on another level you can be a true conformist, and the different parts of yourself are at war. You might not be conscious of it, but most of us are not aware that you are that complex. That you can have fighting parts of yourself.

Tracey: Absolutely. And I think that's where you get multiple personality disorder in its extreme form. It's just comes to the surface.

Raven: Multiple personalities crop up when you are not willing to own it; it's amazing how far people will go to avoid responsibility! That's one area where the Bible got it right. We all have free choice; we choose the life that we want to live. And we are the creators of our lives and of our reality.

Tracey: That's right, and that is even written about in old success manuals, they say that life's greatest rewards are always on the other side of life's greatest frustrations. It's always a testing ground for you. Like what Raven was saying before about trial by fire, or forging the Viking sword, or the saying "The North Wind made the Viking". It's a fine line, because you have to have a certain amount of challenges in your life to achieve, but certain challenges can just be too much and crush the soul. Too much can destroy people. And that's where the line can be drawn by people about what's evil and what's not evil, and what's just people making mistakes. Like that principal of mine in public school; that's just pure evil. To try and turn it around and make me think that there was something wrong with me when I was just simply picking up on the evil that he was doing. But how many kids have that happen to them? I wouldn't have been the only one that got caught in his evil game. He was charged with extortion and it was a big case in the local news. He had threatened all these kids that he would fail them, destroy their lives, all that. I only had the tip of the iceberg.

Daemon: So you were saying, what would I ask other Successful Rebels? What would I be curious about?

Tracey: Yes, keeping in mind that we're trying to help people, we're trying to help outsiders because I know how those people so easily fall through the cracks. And it leads to suicide, it leads to cutting, alcoholism…it leads to a lot of things if no one extends their hand out to the rebels, freaks and outcasts. Maybe they just hear something from one of us, one of their own kind that's successful outwardly at least because we have some money, we have some recognition, we have some nice things, we're happy, so we've done some things that many people aspire to. Let them in on it. Maybe just one thing that any of us say will be the inspiration that reaches someone and gives them hope. We've all been though our shit. All of us. But it's hard to see clearly when you're stuck in the middle of it.

Daemon: Well, it's like Ville, what he was saying…he may be successful on many levels, but he's also got a lot of sorrow and loneliness. Dancing on the razor's edge.

Tracey: Existential angst.

Daemon: So, someone else looking at him while listening to one of his albums will put him on a pedestal, and think "if my life could only be like that." Really? Do you want his sorrow? Do you want his stuff that he has to figure out for himself to be happy? Everyone's got their own shit, and their own good and bad. Don't get caught up envying other people. They have a lot of issues that we don't see.

Tracey: That is a real problem blocking people's happiness. Envy and hero worship, then it can go down the dark road, like stalkers who want you to die because they are so incredibly jealous of you.

Daemon: Well, look at John Lennon and Mark Chapman.

Tracey: Exactly. And look, Lennon had been through so much, with his wife and his career and his family, and then some disturbed person kills him. But I wonder if his spirit knew that going into this life?

Daemon: I believe so. I have chosen now to at least believe that in some way, you chose your family that you're born into, the bullshit that you go through, the time period that you're born into; there's got to be some pattern that makes sense. I refuse to believe that we're in a meaningless existence. I know a lot of people who are successful in the film business, music, whatever, and they are not happy people deep down. So I would definitely have a question to anyone that has reached that level of perceived success in their industry, where they have reached a certain level of fame, I'm always curious about the inner success, the inner development. How has that helped them or held them back? Has it stunted their growth, or is there fear of people wanting a piece of you so much that you start to pull into yourself? I'm lucky, I don't have that level because I'm unknown outside of people that know the world of tattooing. So I can walk down the street, and the worst thing that I suffer is at parties having people asking questions about tattoos, like a doctor or something. Whereas someone really famous, they can't even walk down the street without being accosted. You get into those levels of someone like say, Oprah, and I would so not want to be there.

A lot of artists in general, successful or not, I used to think that if someone's really skilled in some artistic level, that that would mean that there would also be a certain level of spiritual development, and it's totally not the case in a lot of situations. So I'd love to know about that. Where are they at with their trials and spiritual development. No one can say that their ego hasn't jumped in at various times in their lives and gotten in the way, and gotten fluffed up from the attention that you get. And that's when you need to give yourself a reality check, and not buy into your own hype.

∽

Mark Sanborn has chosen to see the obstacles in his life as building blocks, rather than objects that will crush you, or are too large to overcome.

Mark: I think that negative events can create positive outcomes. I was an overweight kid who got picked on a lot. I decided early on that I was going to prove that I was just as good as everyone else and busted my tail to achieve significant things. Rather than become bitter about that aspect of my childhood, I used it to become better.

∽

"Dr. Williams" (an entity channeled by Bart Smit) explains his take on why human beings feel the need for suffering in this lifetime, and why we often willingly choose pain, even if it's on a subconscious level, as a means of growth.

Tracey: Why are people in so much pain? Why do they hurt themselves?

Bart Smit

Dr. Williams: Because human beings don't value evolution unless they've experienced pain. Individuals that have experienced pain, St. Francis' parents...the Catholic Church makes out St. Francis' parents as lovely individuals, but they were tortured individuals that were deeply psychologically disturbed. It is this that has brought St. Francis into his own enlightenment. So when we suffer, we begin to break through what is called the Veil of Duality. We see that darkness or pain in a sense is real, but it indeed is an illusion. And when we liberate ourselves from the pain or the darkness, the confusion or the anxiety or the emotions that imprison people and we liberate or free ourselves, that is when individuals begin to find great success later on in their life. They need to go through that pain to rip that Veil apart. To walk through it.

Tracey: At the same time, as they are dealing with that, rebels seem to have a highly tuned way of seeing the truth in situations, and can spot dishonesty very easily.

Dr. Williams: It's called sensories. The self has sensories, and individuals that travel down the highway of the mainstream don't develop the sensories, and individuals that get off the main road of life, they often have had the difficulties of surviving in the jungle let's say, or the jungle of emotions, they develop this aspect or part of the hypothalamus that cultivates the sensories. The hypothalamus creates emotions, creates chemicals, creates feelings, creates sensories, so the pattern is that we awaken or develop or cultivate sensories within the body that literally tell us, the individual that has experienced great difficulty scans on a constant basis what is happening in their life. A person that lives in the mainstream has not developed the same sensories.

Tracey: So why is it that you find that a lot of those people in the mainstream eventually, whether or not they give the people that function outside of the box a hard time, eventually there is a certain point where it becomes a shift that these people in the mainstream almost look up to the rebels, or put them on a pedestal when the rebel becomes successful.

Dr. Williams: Money. It's all to do with status, power and money. So as the adventurer actually is exploring, he or she gets no recognition. Or any validation. It isn't until he or she is seen to contribute to their life (the mainstream person), egotistic, is where they become recognized.

Tracey: But there's a duality to that, because they actually will try to throw obstacles in that rebel's path.

Dr. Williams: Sure, but part of what they're doing is saying that the calculation, and the equations that you're using should not work. The ones that I'm using should work, so I'm going to pull the carpet out from underneath you because your engineered, designed infrastructure shouldn't be able to sustain itself, so I'm going to pull out the centre beam. But the building doesn't collapse.

Tracey: That's when they become even more aggressive.

Dr. Williams: That is correct.

Tracey: So how does a rebel deal with that? Because there may come a time in their lives where they have to say to their parents or their friends or people in authority "screw you!" I don't buy this anymore.

Dr. Williams: But they do that all along. That's what initiated them. That they don't have to be mainstream, it's their suffering that actually separated them from the need to have that validation. And that is why they become successful.

Tracey: Because they don't care about the judgment.

Dr. Williams: Correct. It affects them, but they are psychologically detached from it. Even though a bad review or a comment can hurt them, it doesn't define them. Those that are on the highway, it defines them.

Tracey: So how does somebody shift themselves, because people can be very sensitive that are like that, and it can crush them, especially as children, you can find that there's almost a tipping point where it either crushes them and they go onto the mainstream, or they throw it off and fully embrace their freakdom, or whatever you want to call it. Is there a word for that axis?

Dr. Williams: Not really. It's a different stage in each individual. And it's not necessarily one thing, it can be an accrual of situations.

Tracey: Is there a tool that they can use to make sure that they can throw off that negative energy? And they can build themselves in a healthy way, as opposed to self medicating or going down that addiction path?

Dr. Williams: That depends upon their social infrastructure. It depends upon their ancestors, their parents, and their karma. It really all boils down to karma.

Chapter 7:
It's Not About the Piercings:
It's About Hard Work

"The two most powerful warriors are patience and time."

- Tolstoy

The Successful Rebel doesn't identify him or herself by the number of piercings or tattoos they have, by their clothing, their mannerisms or their makeup. Success must be backed up by years and years of commitment and dedication to the path you have sought. Any success that is not the result of sustained and vigilant effort is a false accomplishment; it will evaporate as quickly as it materialized.

Each and every one of our Successful Rebels spent years refining their craft, paying their dues, and sticking with it, even when that defied logic. Their internal rudder kept them on course, but they still needed to row.

Tracey: You were telling me before about how you still haven't learned how to drive...and I thought that all of you rock stars had to go out and purchase a sports car immediately after your first success!

Ville: That's the American rock star, right? But rock star is really not an occupation. I consider myself a musician.

Tracey: Yes, that's right.

Ville: Yeah, a rock star is somebody who does a lot of drugs, does a lot of chicks, and behaves like a fucking asshole. That's not really what I aspired to be when I was growing up.

Tracey: That has probably served you well, because some of the super rich that I've dealt with in my life seem to have completely lost perspective on what it means to be a decent person.

Ville: Well, it's a different level when you don't see the tree bearing the fruit of your labor, if you know what I'm saying…you just have a lot of money…and you think that a black Amex, that's the key to the Pearly Gates. Work is the key to the Pearly Gates, not the money. You know, making something, creating something that you feel comfortable with, you know, creating your own puzzle out of yourself, and there's always a piece of that puzzle missing. That's why I'm writing a new song, trying to become whole. The journey is as they say, is a lot more important than getting to the destination.

Tracey: Sure but, there's a certain punk rock sensibility that says that your life has to be that way to create rock and roll, (which I think is bullshit)…

Ville: Again, we have to start speculating upon the fact that a lot of people don't write music because of music. It's like alcoholism, people think it's a disease, I don't believe in that. I believe that there are underlying issues, you just want to dumb down and self-medicate, and feel better. At times, you just want to feel a bit good, and it fucks your life up. So, people do so for many different reasons… you shouldn't live in the streets because you think it's cool, when you don't have an apartment, it's not cool. Obviously, everybody wants to have an apartment, it'd be nice. The money doesn't hurt. It's depending on what your goal is… having money around for me doesn't change the goal. The best thing money can buy is that you don't have to spend eight hours a day at work and then get home and pick up your guitar and work another eight hours, and then sleep two hours and then do the same thing all over again. I never really had to do that since I had not rich, definitely not rich parents, but my parents were giving everything they could for me to do what I wanted. They gave me an ultimatum, basically two years, that they would help me out to get started and then they said please don't drop out of school, but I said I gotta do what I gotta do, and I did drop out when I was maybe fifteen. At that time I wasn't able to get the education that I wanted from school, you know I'd love to go back to school some day and finish it, and maybe study something, but there's too many things to do when it comes to music and I knew what I wanted to do and never had an alternative. I studied music, and maybe I never knew what kind of a band I wanted to sing in or I wanted to play in, or whatever, but I knew that it had something to do with music, and that's what you have to do then. You just have to sacrifice everything on the altar of rock and roll. *laughing*

Tracey: Of course. And that's good, because there's a certain demographic that listens to your music that is kind of the kid in high school that feels like an outcast, feels misunderstood, gets beat up, and I think that your music gives a lot of hope to those kids, to be honest.

Ville: Well you know, music gave me a lot of hope when I was younger. Black Sabbath and all that. I'm a lyrical person more than anything, but I flip the finger to everybody when required. And I never really went along with peer pressure. I think that a good way of giving people the finger is when they least suspect it is to study better than anybody else and still look like a fucking punk rocker. Just show people that looking a certain way, or thinking a certain way, or reading some kinds of books, or listening to certain kinds of music, doesn't mean that you're a degenerate.

Bill Jamieson, our modern day "Indiana Jones" didn't have success fall in his lap – he had to work extremely hard and hustle for everything he has.

Tracey: When you were going through your problems in school, feeling like an outcast, what was it that kept you from giving up?

Bill: I must say I did very poorly in school. Dyslexia was not acknowledged or known about at that time. I was very frustrated, and was unaware of my learning disability, and because of this I went into the workforce at an early age. I was always an overachiever; working late hours and always excelling at all the tasks given to me. I once had the opportunity to take a one-week sales and marketing course by my company. It was total brain washing; ten hours in a room each day. They were teaching you how to turn anything negative into a positive. As much as I hated attending this course, I must say it helped me in my future endeavors. I became a sales manager for a freight forwarding company where the average salesman made four appointments a day, but I would make ten.

Chapter 8:
The Downside:
Drawbacks To Living Authentically

"An honest man is the noblest work of God."

– Alexander Pope

Tracey: Alexander Pope has also been a personal hero of mine, as I think that he personified the Successful Rebel spirit. I learned about him when I was in elementary school, and I appreciated the man and his writings so much that I've named my son after him. My husband's last name is Pope, so the name Alexander was a natural. The quote "Fools rush in where angels fear to tread" is from the writings of Pope. He was a writer and poet in the 1600's, located in England when to be a Catholic meant that you were not allowed to go to school. Pope was from a wealthy Catholic family, and they managed to get his education in a series of back room, secret schools that were run by other persecuted Catholics. Eventually, his family was forced to move to an estate outside of London, because Catholics became banned from living within the boundaries of the city. Alexander Pope became a prolific writer, and he was actually a forefather of the blogger, as he used to write about the society of the day and hold them up to ridicule and expose their corruption. Pope's writings were self-published, and he made a handsome income from the sale of them. If you do any research into Alexander Pope's writings, you will be amazed at how many of his passages are common sayings, even in this day and age. He was a rebel that I greatly admire, as he overcame huge obstacles to let his voice be heard. If he could become a success against all odds, why can't you?

It seems so simple – why doesn't everyone live authentically? If there truly is no one "correct" way of living your life, why aren't more of us casting off the shackles and just letting our true selves out?

It's not always comfortable, and it's not always easy. People are afraid of others that are living their lives according to their own internal guidance system. We've all been raised to toe the line, to pay attention to rules and to follow a prescribed way of being: do well in school, go to university and take something safe like commerce, enter a big company and scale the ladder, get married, have 2.5 kids and buy a house in the 'burbs. And why wouldn't they want you to do this? The typical track makes you a great consumer, a taxpayer, a law-abiding citizen who doesn't have time to cause a problem. Society doesn't care if your soul is suffering, unless that manifests itself in some objectionable behavior, which they will quickly medicate, or incarcerate if the opportunity arises.

We want you to understand that this won't be clear sailing. But it's worth it.

Ville Valo's childhood wasn't what most would consider "typical". His parents owned a sex shop and he spent some time working there, even having the uncomfortable occurrence of having to wait on one of his schoolteachers at the counter.

Tracey: One of the things that I've noticed on my travels, going into the fact that your family owns a sex shop, is the experience that when I was younger I had a few friends that worked as exotic dancers for extra money, and what I really noticed about it was all of a sudden they had a certain stigma that people were judging them. And actually some of the nicest people that I ever met and some of my friends that I still have today came from the adult entertainment industry.

Ville: Sure, yeah, but you know…it's a tough job. It's like being a cab driver, you know? It's very addictive, because you do see the cash in your hand every night. Obviously, depending on where you work. But then again, to be honest with you, if you do go to random, divey strip joints you know, it's pretty sure that there's something illegal going on.

Tracey: Oh absolutely.

Ville: That's the reason, you know, there's a lot of fucking and abuses of all kinds in those kind of places, so that's the reason that people still do stigmatize that…you know… *laughing* Tough luck!

Tracey: That actually never went on where my friends worked, Ville… *both laughing*

Ville: Well, that's good for you, and I know people that actually have worked in high class places, you know that are safe, but still, there's a lot of peculiar characters, and you have to be strong to pull it off…but really, it's not too far from being a musician, you know, all musicians I consider being egocentric, sexaholic, junkies, more or less…doesn't really matter where you come from, so we're trying to change that stereotype one way or the other.

∞

It's not just our careers, or our sense of self that can be injured by trying to live authentically in a world that would prefer we don't. Relationships are frequently difficult to create and maintain for those trying to have an alternative lifestyle.

Dr. Williams shares his insights on why this may be an issue for the Successful Rebel.

Tracey: One of the things that I've noticed is that it's a pattern with a lot of rebels that until they find their own happiness, their love relationships always blow up. How do you express to people that there are times in your life when you're meant to be alone, and find out those things about yourself, because it's a pattern that you're doomed to repeat, over and over again, trying to get into relationships because they're lonely, and it ends up throwing them off their path of where they are meant to be.

Dr. Williams: I don't know if they're going to understand this or not. In the teachings of the Vedas, they speak of what's called the Palace of the Mirrors. And the Palace of the Mirrors is the emotions, feelings, addictions, things that we keep playing out because we perceive that this is our identity, the egoic self. If we don't spend a considerable amount of time by becoming the witness of our thoughts, we can never evolve.

If we're in a relationship, as much the relationship can be challenging, but we keep playing out aspects of our pain body, things of our life story. If we're lucky enough, and we're privileged enough, and we have enough time on our own becoming aware of what we're thinking, and our behavior, and become aware of our stories, and have the ability to get back into the now, of this moment, by re identifying who am I right now, not my story, but where I am this moment, right now, then that's when we become ready to be in a relationship. Because otherwise, we play the same stories, the same pain body, the same scene all over. It doesn't matter who the other person is.

Tracey: So until you honor that within yourself, until you look into that mirror, you aren't ready for a relationship.

Dr. Williams: Right.

Christina Cox has found the demands of acting and being employed in such an unusual industry has been very hard on relationships.

Christina: I don't go out in LA, I don't party, I'm not a scenester. It doesn't mean that I haven't had opportunity to. I've gone to a couple of them and there's just this realization that I'm not the kind of girl that can be lured or cajoled into anything that I don't want to do. I actually require honest conversation. I'm happy having a select group of outstanding friends rather than a whack of acquaintances. So rather than putting myself in a situation where I have to offend someone because I don't want to party with them, I just don't go. Not to mention the paparazzi/tabloid culture and how it thrives on that environment and the people in it. So if and when things really come together for me, it will be on my terms. And again, this is not me judging anyone else's choices. If they're genuinely having a good time out at a club dancing on bars, knock yourself out! It's just not for me. I'm too shy. And clumsy. I'd end up falling off the bar and hurting myself.

Working musicians, especially those that are touring experience one of the most disruptive, relationship killing schedules known to man. Ville Valo knows this all too well.

Ville: I'm occasionally fairly lonely, but let's say the occasional loneliness compared to the purgatory of a dysfunctional relationship…let's say I'm fine with the solitude right now.

Tracey: Absolutely, I completely understand. Being in a bad relationship is torture. I have an ex husband, and it was difficult for quite a while.

Ville: Yes, but it was probably some good times as well, to keep the whole thing going.

Tracey: Of course, but you don't go into it thinking "boy, I'd like to torture myself for a few years, so here I go"…

Ville: Some people do…

Tracey: I guess, but I try to avoid that. Torment doesn't agree with me.

The challenges to living your life authentically will confront you in every area of your existence: your career, your friends, your family and your relationships. Is it worth it? Anything worth having takes time, sacrifice and hard work. The rewards of living a life that you have designed, that you feel passionate about and that you can be proud of will far outweigh any of the challenges we've outlined in this chapter.

It's important that you recognize these challenges when they occur as a normal part of the process, and not a sign that you're on the wrong track.

Chapter 9:
Get Off the Cross:
Rebel Martyrdom

"I am very fond of truth, but not at all of martyrdom."

– Voltaire

Our culture has a long history of glorifying martyrdom; one need look no farther than Jesus Christ to see that those who give themselves up for some greater cause are seen as noble, or more spiritually evolved than those of their community.

But to be honest, we think martyrdom is a complete cop-out. If you really are that wonderful, why would you want to leave the planet? We need you here – not floating around in the clouds.

There are less dramatic forms of martyrdom that include "suffering for your art" and telling anyone who will listen how hard it is to be you. No one chooses your path, you decide it for yourself, so complaining and twisting about how hard it is to be a rebel is the ultimate turn off. And let's face it – complaining is not rebelling. It's whining about the status quo without making any effort to change it.

Tracey: What advice do you have for rebels and freaks, whatever you want to call us, to be successful but want to do it on their own terms?

Sloan: You have to take action, and you have to think differently. You start working for yourself, whether you sell ice cream like those migrant workers who go block to block, I don't care what it is. Or if you're selling pillows and then you become a millionaire, whatever it is, you have to start doing it. You treat it like a business. You have to look at it like a money generating business. You have to assume that it's going to make money, and I don't think that people do assume that. They think "Oh, I'll try it, but I have to have a real job." No, it is your real job. You have to assume that it is, and sometimes yes, you're going to have to borrow money and at some times you may not know where the money is coming from. You may not understand where the money's coming from. But if you take the approach through action that it is your job, it will become that. But it's not easy, because society says you go to school, you get an education, but people with educations can't do what I'm doing. Maybe they have better material things overall, maybe they save their money better, maybe they have better health and dental plans, whatever, but in the long run, they are still losing an element of freedom, and for me, freedom is the most important thing. Freedom to be exactly who I am. Not to follow somebody else's idea of who they think I should be. And so that was the most important thing for me, always. Since I didn't have family that took me in as a part of the clan, to connect to, it gave me the freedom to know that people who are connected to a group of people, that's only one part of reality. Because we all are born alone, and we all die alone. So to learn detachment from being connected to other people, that is actually a blessing. Because you can choose to connect, and you can choose to not take it so personally that if you lose that connection it's not the end of the world. I enjoy that element, and I'm talking even with my kids and my marriage. It doesn't matter to me. If they leave, they leave. I've enjoyed the time that I've had with them. I'm in the moment, and that's that. I don't expect anything different, and I was like that even as a child. I think that benefited me.

Tracey: So you have a detachment that you work with, and that's probably helped you in your work as well, because I'm sure that you see some fairly heavy things with clients.

Sloan: Oh yeah. I work with some murder cases, child abuse cases, people who've been abused as children, which is devastating, drug addiction, suicides...there's a lot of people that commit suicide, although I don't advise it. It's really not worth it.

Tracey: Have you ever had any spirits come through like that? Somebody that died by their own hand? What do they say when they come back through?

Sloan: Nine out of ten times when someone has taken their own life, and this includes drug overdoses, they are remorseful in the instant that they cross over. Within three seconds, I can hear it. They show me, and for me it comes through where I will get the impression that I'm in the middle of their death experience. It's not like I think that I'm dying (although it can get like that at times), it's that they're showing me a piece of the reality of what they experienced. And usually they try to get back into their body. They try to ground in, and the minute that they can't, they become either enraged or hysterical. That's the energy that I feel. I get a migraine headache of the dirtiest nature. It's just a dirty headache, just mind numbing. It's like being socked in the head. They can't believe that they're dead, and it takes them a long time to rectify it. Sometimes it's over quickly, but they can't move on. They don't want to deal with the repercussions of their actions, because they have to process it. They have to look and see how their actions have affected other people.

Tracey: So that's something to remember for people that become full of despair because they want to express whatever in their lives and it doesn't go well and they have failure. If they ever think that things are so bleak that they'd like to kill themselves, they will regret it, one way or another. Correct?

Sloan: They're going to regret it within minutes. Not even minutes, seconds. I've felt it. They've showed me how they died and I can feel them leaving their body, and then when they realize what they've done… I'm talking like a lot of drug overdoses, couple of gunshot wounds immediately regretted what they've done. I mean, as the bullet hits their head. But they can't take it back. Every single time. I've never heard of anyone saying "I'm so glad that I did this!" I had one overdose that told me, and he's the brother of a famous rock singer, and his girlfriend came to me and he was out of his physical pain, but he was mortified that he caused such pain to the people around him, and he was constantly hovering around his mother, because he had seen the pain that he had caused her and it was overwhelming to him. He was devastated by what he'd done, but yet at the same time his physical body was unable to be here. He was physically in pain, just by being alive. Just by his brain chemistry, not necessarily depression, but his brain chemistry was painful to him.

Tracey: Wasn't there an issue with bi polar disorder?

Sloan: I'm not really familiar with him, only when the girlfriend calls me…I have a couple of clients actually that are very connected to him and when they show up he'll come through, but other than that I don't pay attention. Because for me, they become no different than you and I. Any celebrity.

Tracey: Sure. So you have a lot of celebrity clients, but you probably don't want to name them.

Sloan: Lots. A member of the British rock royalty, and his whole family. Lovely family, and they've had their own set of challenges, but fantastic people. And a very famous celebrity. She was somebody who's energy, when she died, she was hell bent on dying. There was an element of both recklessness and suicide. It wasn't really suicide, but it was reckless death. There is a difference…suicide is to murder one's self. In the Ten Commandments, it says thou shalt not kill. Well, you can't kill yourself either. God looks at it the same way. If I kill you, he punishes me the same way if I take my own life. People don't see that. They think they have control. Yes, you have free will, but you are not allowed to do that. We are given the ability to do it, but we are not supposed to choose to do that. With somebody like her, when her son passed away was when she became frantic for answers, which is the case with most people. When somebody they love dies they become frantic. Her son's energy came through quite strongly, but quite passively. He was an exceptionally passive person. He was a person that was not like his mother, let me put it that way. He was, in certain elements like the drug taking, but he was not in other elements. In his level of communication, he was telling me that she was waiting, she was waiting for something. And I knew that in five years, she would be dead. I do feel that the element of the timing was accidental, because she was not supposed to die right then. But within the next five years she was going to pass. They told me that.

Tracey: She was just punishing her body with all the surgeries and all the substances that she was taking at the same time, wasn't she?

Sloan: Absolutely, and after her son died, she was completely out of her body when I communicated with her. She wasn't someone that was physically grounded in her body, even as a client when I was talking to her. I don't mean that she was crazy either, far from it. I just mean that she was disconnected from the fact that she was a physical person. She was completely disconnected from that. She was a person that had a lot of trust issues, issues with childhood. But here's the interesting thing: when she passed over, I got the news from my husband who had just heard it on the radio. I phoned that girl that did the makeup for the body and buried her, who was her girlfriend. She was a very good friend of hers and also her hairdresser and makeup artist. She was the person who dressed the body. Her spirit's energy came through so strongly that she locked us out of our bedrooms, she was in the house trying to get our attention, basically. She was dynamic. I can see why she was a celebrity, she was absolutely dynamic in her energy in death. Really strong, really powerful. A few days before her death I was feeling another death energy, but didn't know where it was coming from. I didn't know it was hers. As soon as she passed, it stopped. I didn't know whose it was however. Even with my own relatives, and with my stepson, I experienced his death, and that happened five years before he died. After the funeral, he came to me and showed me. I will get it beforehand and afterward.

Tracey: So are you saying that they actually show up and say this is what's happening to me, or do you just get this horrible feeling?

Sloan: I'll actually just start seeing it in my head and they'll tell me that I'd better get ready, better get a funeral plot, all kinds of directions like that. They'll show me pieces of it, and then I'll get what I call psychic Tourette's, where I can't stop saying it. I repeat and repeat and repeat. It's like it's getting into my energy, and the closer that it is to the day that it happens, I go a little bit off of my rocker. You know when you go to the zoo and you look at the monkeys? You watch them in the cages and they start jumping up and down? The closer it gets to the incident that I'm feeling, I will start behaving like that. I become crazed with it. I've had that happen. My birth mother passed away in February and the night before she passed away I was sitting in my living room, and I said "oh my God, get me the aspirin, I'm having a heart attack!" And of course, my family looks at me like, whatever, because they hear things like this all the time from me. I freak out and think I'm dying, and it's happening to someone connected to me, and then I find out later. I think it's happening to me and I feel it. So the next morning I get a phone call and that's what she died of. A heart attack. I was feeling it. And she was only sixty, so I didn't think that it was her. I didn't know where it was coming from because it hit me first. And the distressing part is that I don't know that it's not me at the time.

With the death of the famous celebrity, on the Christmas Eve prior, something very unusual happened. I woke up at around two in the morning and went downstairs, and I said to my husband "my God, my leg is swelling up, I've got an infection. I'm in my pajamas and he's looking at it and saying it's fine. And then he took a picture of it, because sometimes you have to show me on a camera. So he showed it to me, and it wasn't swollen. So then we went back to sleep, and I woke up again at four and said to him, "there's no skin on my bones! I can't put my makeup on, my skin is gone!" And he said to me, your face is there. There's nothing wrong with it! And I still thought that it was falling off of my bones. So later on, when she died those symptoms stopped, and a week after the funeral, her friend called me, the friend who was doing her makeup, and she said to me "it has to be closed casket, I can't put the makeup on her face. And that was because they left her in a cooler for a week. Remember all the drama when she died about who would bury her where? So her friend had put pink hair extensions in for her and done all of that, but they couldn't show the body because of the condition. It was so sad. But then I understood that spirit was trying to show me something. It was a prediction, in the middle of it. But it also made me think about something which I'd like to research; I believe that we live simultaneous lives in different dimensions. So actually, her death in my prediction had already happened because I was already at the point where they were trying to put makeup on her face. I just don't know how to split the energy to figure that out.

Tracey: You're talking about something that I've talked about with many different people, and that's the idea in quantum physics that all moments in time exist simultaneously, and we are just tracing a path through, but there's many other pathways at that exact time.

Sloan: Absolutely. I've lived that moment. I lived that moment, I heard those words, I saw the pictures of it in my mind. They were showing me in pictures and putting the words in my mouth. But it wasn't confirmed until about a week later when they had the funeral. And I realized at that moment that for me to pick it up, it had to exist somewhere, in some plane of existence at that time. I was predicting it, but it was through living it verbatim. It was very strange. It was her soul telling me the story of what was going to happen, but it was already happening on some plane of existence. I think that a lot of what happens with me when I begin to pick things up psychically is that my energy floats up and away from the earth, as our energy on earth is very slow, thorough necessity, just to function with day-to-day stuff.

Tracey: So, as soon as spiritually we're off the planet and into the spirit world, do we experience things in a more sped up fashion?

Sloan: Absolutely, because to stay on earth, it needs to be slower; I mean this is why I'm afraid to fly. I've never heard anyone say it to me until this summer when I was in Canada. One of the producers said to me "I love to fly because if you remove the plane, it's just our bodies hurtling through space." And I said that's exactly why I'm afraid to fly. It's the perception of the plane, and I know, if you speed it up, the molecular structure of the metal becomes fluid, therefore, we don't exist in that state. I know that, and it bothers me. We don't exist in that plane. You see, our energy has been densified for us to vibrate on this planet. It's very slow. It's like walking with a bunch of four year olds who are totally slow and you're trying to run a marathon. When you leave the physical body, you lose that density and you're free. It takes a lot to ground us on earth, and psychic people have a hard time being grounded even though we're stuck to the energy of the earth. It's kind of an interesting thing. If you sped up the metal of the plane, it would then become liquid. In others words, if you change the molecular structure of the metal, by heating it, or changing the dynamic of how the particles fit, which would either be like rotating the earth quicker, or more slowly, if you do that, the plane would no longer exist. Flying I know is not reality. I know it's not really there. I'm not really protected in this metal thing, you can go ahead and check the structure all you want, it really doesn't exist. It's something that my mind is saying needs to exist for me to fly.

Tracey: So that freaks you out?

Sloan: Totally. Well, I've learned to live with it. I'm a freak flyer because of that. And I have been since I was a child, it just struck me that the plane was something put there because humans needed it, not because it was really needed.

Tracey: Yeah, I know what you're saying, I don't like flying either.

Sloan: You can do it! I've done it, I've flown a lot lately. I flew eight times in a week a few weeks ago. I was all over the place, shooting a few different TV shows, and by the eighth time I was a nervous wreck, but then I was like, well if I die, I die. I couldn't fight it anymore. When I landed, I was like "hallelujah!" but you know what? What I've learned is that when it's your time, it's your time regardless. That I do believe. I absolutely believe that there's a predestined time to die. Just like it was predestined for me to do this psychic work.

Tracey: Was there a time when you finally just said I'm not going to fight it anymore and this is it for me? I'm just going to keep my nose to the grindstone doing this kind of work? And how long ago was that?

Sloan: Probably about ten years ago. When I hit my early thirties. And of course I did readings in my teens and twenties as well. And then when my stepson passed away I stopped. I stopped everything. I stopped talking to people out loud actually, for two years. I mean I went mute. I lost all of my clients, everything. I couldn't speak. I went completely bananas. Which was something that I wanted to mention about my celebrity client, the urge for her son to pull her over to the other side. And she would pick up on that energy, because she was his mother. She would pick up on it intently, but it was intense, she couldn't help but want to die. I've heard this from so many people that have lost children. There's a feeling of "I have to be with them" and you don't quite know how to cope with that, because on earth you're thinking that they're in a grave, so how do you be with that? So you wear their clothes, you do whatever you have to do, but for women in particular, they tend to want to die. They tend to want to cross over, although they don't analyze it like that. They won't tell you that they want to put a gun to their head, because that's more of a male way of dealing with grief, but they feel like that. When my stepson passed it took me two years not to kill myself. And I had a very young child with me, but it was extremely difficult because I could hear my stepson on the other side. I told people about it, which makes them think that you're crazy, but I really felt that I had to kill myself, because he was trying to talk to me from the other side so strongly. I could feel his cries for me to come and help him. That was a very hard lesson to learn, because in the confusion I felt that my ten month old was fine without me, but a grown man who was my stepson and close friend would need me. It was an overwhelming pull. For two years I didn't speak, and literally spoke only in my head. I was lucky that I was able to process it finally and emerge stronger than before. I learned a lot. But it was a two-year trial for my family, because I was just not connected to them mentally. I was completely shut down, and I was caught between two worlds. I think what might have saved me was running. Movement, and it was obsessive. I would run and run, but in other ways I was not responsive in my body. You could tap me and I wouldn't feel it. It was absolutely overwhelming. And my husband had to parent me after that.

Tracey: But maybe it was the whole karmic lesson of how much pain you caused and how much further pain that you could have caused if you didn't get off drugs.

Sloan: That's exactly what it was. And also the guilt of him passing and me not. And I knew it, mind you. I was pregnant with my little son, and spirit told me "this son will be born within the same month as that son, and this son is here to finish that son's lesson. They told me that. So when you're first pregnant and nobody's dead and you're telling people that, they're looking at you like you're crazy. It was horrendous. For me, it was very hard to connect with the physical. You would have sex with me and I couldn't feel it. I carried on in that sense, I brushed my teeth, I did things that I needed to do, but I had no feelings. For a psychic person, it's very hard to stay in the grounded element. And my oldest son became very open psychically during this time; he connected with his brother in spirit and was able to communicate with him and tell me about it. It was all part of our development. And a lot of it was karma and part of our lessons here on earth, and we had to learn to eventually embrace it as such and not to take it so personally. But it was a very difficult lesson to learn. It was insane, really. Just to have that information told to you by spirit and to know that it's going to happen, it was hard. I was off by two weeks in the timing, it actually happened two weeks before I thought it would. For them to tell you, and for you to tell other people without them believing you, and then for you to get crazy and jump up and down like a monkey in the zoo, people really don't understand that. They all think that you're a whack job.

Tracey: Yeah, but at least you're using your super powers for good instead of evil! And now, what do you think of the karma of someone like a famous male movie star, who passed away accidentally right before his movie opens, and it has the biggest opening weekend ever. What's the story behind that?

Sloan: You know what? He was in the same age as my stepson…twenty-seven turning twenty-eight. That is your Saturn Return, and in astrology people die in that time frame because they refuse out of stubbornness to change the way that they're living their life.

Tracey: Isn't that the age when all the rock stars, Janice Joplin, Hendrix, Cobain, Morrison, isn't that when they all died?

Sloan: That's right, Saturn Return! And a famous rock star, I communicated with him quite a bit from the other side. I was teaching a class in 2003 and the class would pick a celebrity topic. So I tried to connect with the energy of him and a famous child murder victim. Remember when they arrested that guy in Asia and flew him back here? He said that he killed her? I predicted that, and I also predicted that he wasn't the one that did it. I also predicted that they would find the guy on the East coast and that he was a family friend. It's coming up soon. They cleared the family, but I feel that they'll catch the guy soon, and it's the dad that's going to make the connection. But it's somebody that they knew. They let him into the house. With the rock star, he told me that he lay there for six or seven hours before he died. In a complete state of fear that he wouldn't die. He wanted to die, and he was stuck in the mindset of somebody who had made this choice, and they were not allowing him to die.

Tracey: So what did he say after that? Was he upset that he had done it?

Sloan: Very much so, and misses his family very much. Feels relieved to be out of his physical body, however. He was a person who I don't think really meshed well in the physical. He physically didn't do well in his body. He had a really bad digestive problem that gave him horrible pain, and when I connected with his energy, his mind was very tortured. He knew how intuitive he was, through his writing. The physical pain that he had with his body had a lot to do with an injury that happened when he was born. He was never diagnosed, but that's what he showed me. He had a valve in his stomach that was open, but shouldn't have been open. It kind of healed on its own, but not in the correct way. He also told me at the time, he took his life not because anyone wanted to him to get straight, but because musically, they wouldn't let him express himself the way that he wanted to. He lived for his ability to live his life and express himself the way that he wanted to. They wouldn't let him do that, and that's why he took his own life. His manager phoned to say that he had read the article about my reading of this, and it was accurate. I felt with him, he made a choice that was based on his ability to control his own life, other than what the media said about his drug addiction. Which was huge, but he couldn't control his own life, that was more the issue. It was an issue of being able to create the way that he wanted to. It had all gotten out of control. They wouldn't let him do what he wanted to do. And now I don't feel that he's around anymore, he's happy in spirit. When people cross over, and they've killed themselves, my understanding is that you've got one of two things. I can either acknowledge what I've done, which means a processing of what I've done, so it would be the equivalent of going before the parole board and listening to how what you've done has affected people in your life, or I can keep around the ethers in the astral level because when you kill yourself, and this I've heard from spirit: you're going to be born right away into another body. So that's why a lot of suicides don't cross over right away. They know that. For example, if you had an issue like you're born into a family and you're a gay kid, into a staunch religious family and you've got some issue with that, and it makes you feel so bad because they're calling you names and your life is tortured from it, if you kill yourself in this situation, you're coming right back as another gay kid. It's going to be the same issues, just expressed through different souls. You will come back, or so they tell me.

Sloan has seen and heard things that few people have, or would want to. The recurring theme from these "suicide ghosts" is that it's a mistake to take your own life. There is no peace in this decision, and for the most part you will either be doomed to mull over this mistake, or will immediately be put right back into the very same situation you're trying to escape. The only way out, it seems yet again, is through.

∞

Raven Rowanchilde, wife of tattoo artist Daemon Rowanchilde has experienced a great deal in her eventful life and now tries to help others through the instruction of Yoga. We spoke with both of them about choices in life.

Raven: Life is all about choice. You can choose to be fucked up, or you can choose to channel your energy or your anger, or you can choose to play the game better. You don't have to become a victim, or an aggressor. You can just be. Judgment is all around us. Judgment is how the diet and beauty industries survive and thrive. And you can either buy in or opt out, as each moment unfolds.

Tracey: Well, that's how I feel about tattoos. I feel that tattooing my body is another way to make it more beautiful, without buying into the traditional values. And I think that it's constructive, because I'm doing it with a positive intent. So Successful Rebels don't give a damn. I'm not sure if it was Crowley or someone from the Golden Dawn, but they said, "that which you desire, desires you." The desires are there to tell you what you need to do in your life. It's also about growing up believing some of the writings of Vonnegut, who said, "All moments in time exist simultaneously." Steven Hawking territory.

Daemon: I think that's because what you're attracted to are parts of yourself, your wholeness that you haven't quite manifested yet…pieces of the puzzle, disguised as separate things.

Raven: It's important to remember that the rebellion is an important part of the process, but you can't get trapped in that victim situation so that you become hooked on the rebellion…at some point you just need to let it go and live.

Tracey: Well, if you want to look at a very high functioning Successful

Rebel, that would be Richard Branson. He rebelled against the idea that you have to be an expert in something before you go into business with it. He just learns about a business for three months and then launches into it with both feet. So the essence of a rebel is someone that will always push those boundaries, in one way or the other. They won't ever swallow the party line, and why should they?

Daemon: One of the tools that we carry is the ability to rebel when we need to. It's really important to have the ability to discern the important issues from ones that we should just look at and then let go of.

Tracey: Living your life without pushing yourself into that mould. Letting your freak flag fly and just being whoever you are; there are so many people who want to do that now. They feel rudderless. They are always feeling like the oddball in everything they do.

Raven: But that's the problem. They're always identifying with the oddball. See, there's a catch 22. If we identify as an oddball, instead of honoring it as a gift, or intelligence or clear sight or whatever, then they will always handicap themselves.

☉

The official definition of martyrdom is: "any experience that causes intense suffering" – let's face it, life has enough challenges and hurts all on its own. There's no need to go out and seek pain and suffering.

None of us can avoid the trials and tribulations of life – the key is not to seek them out, but rather to interpret and learn from those that come to us naturally.

The greatest waste of all is when a life is ended before its time. There is no reason, in our estimation, for making a choice that will leave you, and those around you, eternally tormented.

Chapter 10:
The Enemy

"Rebellion against tyrants is obedience to God."

- Benjamin Franklin

As if there weren't enough internal obstacles to contend with, we must acknowledge that there will be people that wish to block, change or thwart your desire for rebellion from the norm. They will range from well-intentioned, but ultimately frightened, relatives, friends and associates to those that truly do not wish to see others succeed. Whenever a member of a pack decides to do things differently than the group, it engenders a certain amount of anxiety. What will this mean? How will this reflect on me? And perhaps most importantly – "if they do this will it mean I have to confront my own issues?"

Family might seem like the most difficult to deal with on this front, because for most of us, the desire to be liked and included in our own family is always very strong. The idea of disappointing our parents, no matter how old we get, can be a very major deterrent. So how does one deal with the skepticism and disdain of their family group? The same way that we deal with our friends – believing in what we're doing and approaching this with love, but a healthy amount of detachment from their "good opinion". This is much harder than it appears, but it's perhaps the most important fight you're going to have to enter. The lessons you learn from practicing this "loving detachment" will also stand in you in good stead against those less "well intentioned" people that will block your path.

Neev, who we introduced earlier, is fighting both public perception and the law to bring relief to a group of people that are suffering. How could something so noble possibly encounter the amount of blowback that

Neev has encountered? The political hot potato of medical marijuana is a difficult subject for some people to accept.

Neev: My business could never be as big as it could be if cannabis were legalized. If it were legalized, I'd have one office in each province.

Tracey: That's right, I never thought about that. But isn't that why the corruption of organized crime that is growing, they want to keep it that way? Their job is over if it's legalized.

Neev: For sure. It's a form of currency. So right now, guns are being traded for cannabis or cocaine. So now, if it becomes legalized, they've got one less currency to work with. And it's an easy currency to obtain. If it were legalized, it would cost a specific amount to grow, and a specific amount to market... and that's for high quality cannabis. It would be affordable for most people, like a fine cognac or port. In this environment, it's overvalued by ten times as much. So why is this currency so inflated? People benefit from it. You have government, or private enterprise or organized crime responsible for production and sale. And having organized crime in charge of it is the worst of all scenarios, but that's what we have.

Tracey: Until the legalities change, yeah. So, kids that are growing up today, the rebel, the misfit, the outcast, someone doesn't want to deal with school but wants success on their own terms, however that may be. Are there any encouraging words you have for them?

Neev: Any words to the young? Late teens to early twenties and thirties, the time when you don't know when to shut your mouth and you just pop off about everything and the next thing you know you're in huge trouble that has ramifications that are far reaching. Be careful with that. As far as the cannabis industry, it's very hard to be successful, but I have a dream. So I would say to any rebel who has a dream, follow your bliss!

Tracey: So you don't get up and feel that going to work is a struggle?

Neev: Well, it has its moments...but I enjoy what I'm doing.

Tracey: Do you feel that you're doing what you're meant to be doing?

Neev: Yes, but I always want to try new things. It's what life is all about.

Tracey: Okay, so back to words of encouragement for all the rebels. For people who want to live outside the box. Do you feel that you're happy?

Neev: Yeah, but you have to have a certain amount of success to finance your rebellion. All rebellions need money, even the rebels from Star Wars.

Tracey: Was there a time when you made the realization that to further what you wanted to do with your life, you had to use the tools of the establishment?

Neev: Yes, to create success from rebellion. Which is key.

Tracey: When did you come to that realization?

Neev: While I was smoking cannabis! Calm is a California style medical cannabis club. What that means is that the concept started in California. I read about it in a High Times magazine. It was something that I knew that my skills and personality would do well at. That was in 1991. I was in university at the time. I was taking theatre management. Budgets and schedules.

Tracey: So you're saying that basically you have to use the tools of the establishment to create change. You can't do it without money.

Neev: Yeah, every project requires resources. I can't imagine an all volunteer, zero pay charity. Maybe in a cult, where you're working for a religious leader. People have to live.

Tracey: That is the point that most rebels go through, usually in their late teens, early twenties where they have a rebellious nature and as young adults or children they just rebel. And damn the torpedoes, you never know what's going to happen, right? And there comes a time where they choose their path. They see that they need to use the tools of the establishment, to further their cause, or they go completely off the rails. It's like a fork in the road, and people can choose either path at any time. I see rebels that push themselves into the suit, the tie, the button down bullshit, and then they go off the rails with hookers or drugs, drinking, whatever it is…they self-destruct.

Neev: Like a certain US Governor with hookergate…

Tracey: Yes. Then there's the US Senator with the toe tapping in the men's bathroom. It turned out that he was cruising in there. And he was totally against homosexual's rights. And the worst thing about the US Governor was that he crusaded against prostitutes and johns, and he had many tough laws passed, and it turned out that he was a high spending john! So that is another form. They were obviously pushing themselves down into a mould of their own making that caused them to just self-destruct, because they weren't being authentic with themselves. So people have to remember that they have to be authentic with themselves. They might be freaky, they might be gay, they might be an eccentric. There are all kinds, and who are we to judge others or ourselves? If you're being an authentic person and you're a good person, and you're doing these things with people that want to be there with you, then go for it! Let your freak flag fly because life's too short! If you try to push yourself into this bullshit square mode it just blows up in your face. That's why I'm writing this book, because I've looked for a book like this and you can't find one. Alternative people, we don't have many role models.

Tracey: Speaking of being an eccentric, I went through a difficult period where I was consumed with worry when my son was born. I think that having a child, the biggest thing is that you go from only really thinking about yourself, to having someone that you would kill for, throw yourself in front of a train, jump in and drown to save without a second thought. And it's that huge shift in your consciousness that I think blows you away for a few years. I mean, I was a real wreck. I was worried about my son all the time when he was a little baby. It actually gave me panic attacks for the first six months. It was the realization that suddenly you've got someone that you'd do anything for. And it takes a while to get over. You become like a hypochondriac, but for that child's safety. It was through the teachings of Dr. Williams that I overcame this issue, but I was acutely aware at that time about the "us and them" scenario of we rebels and our struggles against the establishment. Dr. Williams' explanation focused on the eternal struggle between the rebels, who he called the Children of the Gods and Goddesses, and the Reptiles, who he described as the spiritually less evolved. For rebels to find success, he explained that you have to use the tools of the establishment, because you will always run up against those people who are Reptiles. Those people are brought into your life for you to change and grow and go onto your path, because with no challenges on your path, you would never do anything. You would just sit back and "fart through silk", your whole life. That's why they're there, for us to lift ourselves out of the situation and be the observer, so that we see our chess moves, and so that we don't go off the rails and rage, or flip out, or freak out. Like many of the celebrities do in Hollywood, but they do it very publicly. The rebels need to stand up and operate authentically. Be honest! If you're attracted to somebody that's overweight, or maybe you prefer someone that's tattooed and super skinny, don't be ashamed to say it, because there's somebody for everybody to love. The regular media has told us that only slim girls are pretty, or only muscled guys are good looking, and it's bullshit. What you're in love with is the spirit, to be honest. You have to like the outer package, but if you like huge boobs and a big butt, be honest about it and let your freak flag fly. Who are we to judge? There's every single type of person on this earth, and they all need support and love. There's too much judging going on in this world. A lot of it is being done in a very corrupt manner, because what it's doing is trying to force people into a mould so that it can sell stuff to them. And perception is reality, unfortunately.

So what about those people outside your circle – religious figures, politicians, business leaders, teachers? How do you deal when you encounter those that aren't working from a place of authenticity and love? How does a Successful Rebel deal with those operating from a place of hate, exclusion and corruption?

Tracey and Ville discussed this in the realm of organized religion. It must be noted here that we don't have a problem with religion whatsoever. Live and let live is our motto. The issue that we have is with religions that use their beliefs as a weapon to dominate others who don't have the same beliefs, and to make people feel bad about themselves because they don't live up to that religion's so called standards.

Tracey: Many organized religions, the whole point is to take away freedom so that you can control and have a docile bunch of people that you can deal with. And I don't mean spirituality, I mean religion.

Ville: That's what religion was turned into. Because of greed. We know the Pope is all about control. How can you call a rock and roll band satanic, and then say "I want to worship the Pope!" "Hail Pope!!"

Tracey: *laughs* You're right!

Ville: And then they could get tattoos of the Pope, and that is the next level.

Tracey: I agree. By the way, my husband's last name is Pope.

Ville: Excuse me?

Tracey: My husband's last name is Pope.

Ville: *laughs* Oh my God, I would make so many jokes out of it!

Tracey: And my last name is Cox.

Ville: Well, you know, you could come up with a few things with that as well…

Tracey: Listen, anybody whose last name is Cox, when you're a young child, you lose all innocence very quickly, because the jokes just happen, you can't help but have them in your face…

Ville: Well, you know, it builds character, doesn't it?

Tracey: My son, I named him Alexander, so his name is Alexander Pope. Have you ever read any of Alexander Pope's writing?

Ville: I just know the name, but no, I haven't read any Pope. But now I'm thinking about kids, since you mentioned your son. Trying to figure out a way, when they're in a tough situation, to be in a responsible way, to be able to free their souls. Through creativity, and more left of centre originality that they need to express.

Tracey: Exactly. I had to remove my son from the school that that he was in, because they told me that there was something wrong with him because he was interested in and questioning death. And then when a class was so dull he told the teachers that he wanted to kill himself because the class was so boring, they decided that he needed to go to the school psychologist. I said that I'd be damned if they did that, because of the experience that I went through. He's going to a holistic school now, and it's amazing.

Ville: Is it based on Rudolph Steiner?

Tracey: It is kind of like the Waldorf schools, which I believe are based on Steiner's teachings.

Ville: Because they have really freaky things as well. I was just discussing with somebody that was thinking about sending their kid over to the Steiner schools, we call them, and I was saying that the only problem with that is why do you want to send a freak amongst the freaks? It's the same as sending a normal person amongst the other normal people, it doesn't make any sense. I really do think that the main thing that school is good for is the fact that you see the social structure that you're going to be fighting against, and with, for the rest of your life.

Tracey: That is a good point. I never thought of that. To change the subject, you haven't been married yet, have you?

Ville: Excuse me?

Tracey: You've managed to dodge the bullet so far, haven't you?

Ville: It's not a very usual thing of people getting married here. I have a few friends who are married here, but I don't know the reason for being married, other than a big party. It's like, what the fuck? You can have a big party anyway!

Tracey: So most people in Finland just live together?

Ville: Some of my friends are married, some of my friends just live together. My mom and dad are married, but they're old school, and they got married back when it was just considered to be the right thing to do. But I would want to have a big church wedding, but I can't since I'm not baptized.

Tracey: What do you mean? You can still have a big church wedding if you're not baptized!

Ville: I guess you can't here. You have to be a part of the church to reserve a church for your wedding, since it's happening under the name of God, right? You can't go into a church and have a satanic ceremony. *both laugh*

Tracey: Or how about a pagan ceremony, and hand fasting where you jump the broom?

Ville: Well, if I speculate upon that, maybe I'll get married in the Vatican so basically I'll be on both sides of the fence, right?

Tracey: Yeah, I'm sure he'll welcome you with open arms.

Ville: Yeah, something like that.

Tracey: I went to an all girl school when I was in high school, and I drove the priests crazy, because number one, I wasn't baptized, so I was going to go to limbo when I died, wherever the hell that is…

Ville: Uh, that's cancelled. I think the new German Pope just cancelled limbo a few months ago. There was a big speculation because they didn't really know where babies go that were there.

(Tracey's note: As an example of what a sweet and thoughtful person Ville Valo is, he researched this information after our interview, and confirmed that it was reported in 2007 that the theological idea of the limbo of infants is not valid in the eyes of Pope Benedict XVI.)

Tracey: Yes, that's where the priests were going to have me filed, so I would have to get a transfer, is that right, into another area?

Ville: *laughs* Yeah, I don't think it's theologically solid to believe in different layers of hell, so basically it's just a fireplace and then a place upon the clouds. And let's say the Christian idea of heaven is my idea of hell.

Tracey: You mean where you have to sit on a cloud and you just worship God?

Ville: Yeah, and play the fucking harp! If I ever go to heaven I hope that I'm going to be deaf, dumb and blind, so we'll see what happens.

Tracey: Yes, we'll all see once we get over there. You know for me, in school, I wasn't baptized, but I was always the one that used to get the highest marks in ethics class and it used to drive the priest out of his mind, because I could parrot back all that nonsense…

Ville: That's the whole thing! That's what I'm saying, what we were talking about considering the creative kids not finding their own place. Use the same weapons! Use the same tools as them. When you have to prove yourself, when you have to prove your cause, or your worth. And that's the problem with a lot of ultra right wing politics. They don't fucking have the intellect.

Tracey: But they think they do.

Ville: And that's why they're so small, and that's why they're so idiotic.

Tracey: We have that kind of problem in Canada right now. We have a mini George Bush Prime Minister named Stephen Harper, and my God. We're very liberal normally. For some reason, we have a bunch of people in Alberta, which is a western province with all the oil now, and they have the political clout now because of the oil, so we've got this guy from Alberta as our Prime Minister. A lot of Canadians are not happy with the current situation.

Ville: That's the way it is. For whatever the atom bomb is that hits your city, you know whether it be God, money, whatever kind of religion, it still hits your city. It's bull, and it's terrible, but as long as it doesn't really affect your everyday living you can consider yourself lucky. As opposed to being in countries where it's not so liberal to say what you mean, to write what you feel, and all that. So in that we have to consider ourselves lucky.

Tracey: You're right. Really, Canada is still a great place.

Ville: And so is North America. I find it fascinating. There are so many possibilities. And the roots are all over the place, it's fascinating. It's like a big candy store. It's fascinating to meet so many different kinds of people. So many different kinds of beliefs. And so many are open-minded as well. Lots of closed minds too, but you know, it's not like the intellectual elite in Europe, feeling superior.

Tracey: Do you feel a difference with the fans, over here as opposed to Europe? Are they crazier here? What are they like? What's the difference?

Ville: People in North America are really straightforward and they ask questions, and that's good. They don't necessarily have opinions, they're not opinionated before they meet you, and that's good. They have open minds, and that's a great thing to have. You know, you don't have to agree with me personally to like our music. Most of the time I don't know what it's all about either, so I just go with the flow and sing the songs. And enjoy it, as much as I can.

Tracey: I appreciate that, but in business, I've found that a lot of North American business people can be very two faced, and very nice to your face but very cruel behind your back if you don't agree with them. At the same time, they'll very happily steal your ideas and take credit for them if they think it will further their careers. Or not only that, you'll find people that will hang around for a while, you know, psychic vampires, or whatever you want to call them…fair-weather friends.

Ville: But at the end of the day, backs are made for stabbing.

Tracey: They seem to be, absolutely.

Ville: That kind of comes back to morals, doesn't it? Same as in art, or music, you know, you listen to the music that you love and then you kind of rip off ideas from your idols, and create some kind of glorious mess out of the ripping off, by accident or on purpose, you create something that is considered to be at least slightly unique. So at the end of the day as an artist, you have to be a psychic vampire as well to absorb and suck in all the information that you can to express yourself better.

Tracey: Sure, but there's taking influences and then there's outright plagiarism and outright ripping off.

Ville: I do understand that, but that's when it comes down to morals. More or less, it's about where you draw the line.

Tracey: It's about the corporate suits, too. Unfortunately, my experience is that in business, I've always been an open book, because that's the way I live my life, most of the time, I mean. I don't give a hundred percent of my secrets, as you know, but these corporate suits, they'll sit there and they'll chat with you…"oh tell me about this, what you're doing, oh, isn't that interesting…" And then they'll steal your ideas.

Ville: In Europe, it's not as bad. I know it's very windy on top, and a lot of the dudes there are very afraid of getting the boot. If you do business with any American, you rarely get an answer, yes or no, which you always do get with a European. In America, you always have to go through, assistants and assistants and assistants, and nobody is able to say yes or no. And that's one of the reasons that lawyers make so much money in that country, because they are the ones saying, at the end of the day, yes or no to a particular question, whatever that might be. Indecisiveness seems to be the business disease, at least in America. In Europe, it's always been a lot more straightforward. You know, if you ask for something, if you ask whether this is considered to be a good idea or not, you're given an answer and not a lot of bullshit. You waste a lot of time by bullshitting, and we don't have a lot of time. So, I'm always usually straight to the point.

Tracey: Sure, you're just more blunt, which I like, personally, because I'm the same way. Whether or not people believe that I'm a bitch, or whatever they want to call me in business because I'll just flat out say what I think.

Ville: Yes, but by that you save a lot more time to be able to enjoy life by sitting with your friends and drinking red wine. In that sense, I've never understood the socializing mixed with business. To a certain extent I do understand, you know if a deal's gone well and you want to sit down and have a dinner and congratulate everybody for work done well, that's understandable, totally, but while doing the business, there's ridiculous amounts of bullshitting, and ridiculous amounts of indecisiveness.

Tracey: But is it indecisiveness, or is it somebody saying, "well, I don't know…" and then they go down and steal your ideas and say that they came up with it.

Ville: Well, let's say there's a lot of people taking credit when you have succeeded, and then washing their hands of it when you haven't. I think that if you work hard, even if the fruit of your labor would be condemned as being a failure, still you have worked hard and it doesn't take the work away. It's not just about kicking the ball in the goal, it's about working to get there. It's about rehearsing, it's about getting yourself in the right state of mind, you know, as we talked about last time, getting there is a very important process.

Bart Smit, or rather his counterpart, Dr. Williams, sees the struggle as a much larger, metaphysical battle that is just an intrinsic part of the human experience:

Dr. Williams: Those Reptiles as I call them, those people come from this place, from this particular planet. There's a density, so that when you have a conversation with them, it's like "didn't you and I have this particular conversation yesterday?" There's a density, and there isn't a deep sense of recognizing the inner self, they only identify with what's called the small self. And so the inner self is the part of us that's in divine union with God, and the small self is the egoic self, which means that we constantly identify with our ego, and the ego says "I want this sandwich, and I want that purse, and I want that car" and the ego continuously gains control so that the individual doesn't liberate themselves from the egoic self. And then there are people that, when you connect there's this instant connection, and the majority of these people don't come from here. The majority of them come from the 12th planet, and sometimes that's called Children of the Gods and Goddess, and they find their own way, and they find their own path. And they don't have, well, 99 percent of them don't have business plans. They all are inspired by a vision that they can hold and sustain, without needing to follow the actual steps that lead them from A to B, they will actually just ingrain the entire experience within their entire body. And then there's a Reptile, which is like an alien formation of a human being, and they have this innate ability to dismiss anything and everything around them. Usually politicians, like George Bush, he's a great Reptile. You can see that he has no remorse or consequences. He doesn't register these layers of emotions where most people have a deep conscience, they don't have a conscience, and they can be very predatory, they can make a lot of money, they can become very wealthy, they are very dismissive of everything around them, they have no sense of following through on promises to people, they are very on the surface and lip service, and you have a deep sense of "oh my God, this guy genuinely cares", has an innate ability to fool individuals, to think that there's an empathy within them, but there's none. Hitler had that innate ability. And so if you look at all the bankers, billionaires, the majority of them are those innate reptiles.

Tracey: So is it a fight between the two? Is there some kind of a karmic fight between the two energies?

Dr. Williams: Well, that's exactly what's happening, and the world is beginning to shift. How can you go from Atlantis to the Stone Age? How can you go backwards? So human beings have lost the axle. They've allowed the emotions to identify them, the chemical reactions in the brain to identify us, and emotions are chemical reactions that happen in the brain. Emotions are simply there to tell us what's happening at that moment. A person that is a rebel, or someone from the 12th planet, has an innate ability to observe instead of absorb, and observe the emotions that are originating from their mind, but they don't necessarily become absorbed or consumed by the chemical reactions. They are constantly analyzing or assessing "how do I do this differently?" Emotions can affect them by influencing some of their decision-making, but predominantly they have this innate ability to step outside the box and become the witness of the mind, and they don't allow themselves to be absorbed by the actions of the mind, or the emotions of the mind.

Tracey: I also find that what you're saying is true, even when they are children, because you see the incredible amount of torture that it puts a lot of children through that have that witnessing and knowing ability, knowing that something is wrong, dealing with those reptilian people that they want to rebel against, and fight against it, and they don't have the skills yet in that body.

Dr. Williams: So, if you look at the cultural evolution, if you look at Bill Clinton's campaign, it worked, because it was based on emotions and fear, and people reacted to that. Now you've got, 8 years later, and you've got his wife who uses the same tactics, except people are saying, "your judgment and your politics are not acceptable". It's not working anymore. Culturally, people have shifted, and they're not allowing the media or their mind, and that's because they're starting to watch movies like "What the Bleep Do We Know" and "The Secret" and "Conversations with God" which have shown people that their emotions are not their identities.

The best advice the people we interviewed offered was this: you are going to encounter people on your path that want to derail you, either because they love you and are afraid for you, or because they are trying to block or steal your power. Recognize these encounters for what they are – checkpoints that allow you to constantly re-examine what you're doing and why. If you know you're being authentic to yourself, loving to the world and you're not hurting anyone – rock on!

PART 3

Chapter 11:
There Is No Spoon:
Don't Take No For An Answer

"All things appear and disappear because of the concurrence of causes and conditions. Nothing ever exists entirely alone; everything is in relation to everything else."

- Buddha

Melissa: The concept that "there is no spoon" seems to be a very rare and valuable idea to grasp. When I saw The Matrix in 1999, this particular observation really struck me. What they are essentially saying is that all limitations are self-imposed, because the only version of reality that we have is the one we create. Now we're not saying you can walk in front of a bus and have it pass through you (although quantum mechanics tells us that that is possible, it's just not very likely).

Rather than seeing obstacles, Successful Rebels see opportunities, or frankly nothing at all. Instead of deciding what can't happen, they just go forward, knowing they will do what they need to do. They don't have to "fight the system", they just pass through it.

We see this in entrepreneurs that go from rags to riches on a simple idea, in astonishing musical talents that don't fit the mould of what the "package" looks like, in the unlikeliest of heroes. In his first month in office, Barack Obama has decided to take on a crippling economic crisis, the war in Iraq and Afghanistan, universal healthcare and even the cure for cancer! It's not that Successful Rebels have some superhuman ability to surmount obstacles – they simply do not see them, or they choose to ignore them and forge ahead.

Tracey: Ernie Boch Jr. is the number one Honda and the number three Toyota dealer in America. He is also the most outrageous marketer in the automotive industry today, and what he does works. Ernie is an inspiration to every rebel that wants to let his freak flag fly and do things outside of the box. For Ernie Boch Jr., the road less traveled has been the path to fame and fortune.

Ernie Boch Jr. Photo credit: Rebecca Gauchman

Tracey: What was the biggest obstacle for you to overcome when you wanted to assert your individuality in your business, because if you go on your website "Save a Rockstar" or some of your advertising, it's completely different from anything that anybody's done in the car business, so I wanted to know, I'm sure you had naysayers...

Ernie: Oh yeah! Well...what was the biggest thing that I had to overcome? Well, I don't think of it as overcome, I really didn't have anything to overcome, I just did it!

Tracey: You just did it. So, you're obviously a person that doesn't care what other people think, then.

Ernie: No...well, I care what other people think as to how I will, or if it will affect them. Like, you know, I don't run around with an axe and chop off people's heads...you know, I care that they think that they're safe with me, but I don't care what people think of what I do because I don't feel that they understand it the way I do.

Tracey: That makes sense. But I know from the aspect of being a car dealer's kid, any time you step out of that box of the way that they thought about your parents or your dad, or whoever, did you not have people that questioned your way of doing business?

Ernie: Oh I had negative people, and I had some negative responses, but the overall response was very positive. With everything that I do.

Tracey: So, even the things that are really out there...

Ernie: Yeah, I was in the paper the other day, in the gossip columns, and I did a commercial, I dressed up as a waitress and it was in complete, full character, and my mother gave me some crap, and my wife gave me some crap, but you know, overall it was okay! *laughs*

Tracey: *laughing* Yeah, I've seen that on YouTube and it's hilarious. I love it! And I'm sure that it attracts attention in a good way too.

Ernie: Right, yeah!

Tracey: So, basically, you didn't find that you had a lot of obstacles thrown up that way.

Ernie: No.

Tracey: That's good, because a lot of rebels do. A lot of people that I've interviewed have had that happen.

Ernie: But I think that it's their perception! If somebody throws up an obstacle, they see it as an obstacle. I don't see it as an obstacle.

Tracey: Do you just see it as a challenge?

Ernie: No, I don't see it as anything! I don't care what they say! It doesn't affect me at all!

∞

Christina Cox has struggled with "there is no spoon" because the film industry sometimes appears to thrive on telling people what isn't possible. It's deeply ironic, as the system is founded on the idea of dreams coming true, but it's also very challenging.

We talked with her about success – something it seems actors are very reluctant to admit, and the obstacles that have been, it seems, frequent.

Christina: I know that you don't manifest wealth if you're living in a poverty state of mind. And by that I mean prosperity in all areas, not just financial. But it can be pretty hard to create that energy of prosperity when you're feeling low.

Tracey: Everyone's going to screw up somewhere, and that's the thing for people to keep in mind. We're all the same. We all have obstacles.

Christina: Sure, but I think that if you're going to use the film industry as an example, if you're going to go off the rails, they had to have been pretty successful before. You can't be a mediocre to middling, minor celebrity. What would you make your comeback from? There's an actor (I'll leave it to you to figure out who I mean) but he is so incredibly talented I could watch him read the phone book. But he had his demons (as so many do) and he screwed up. But he was also really, really well established when he screwed up but knowing how talented he was, of course you want to see him have a comeback. It's different than Jane Q. Public, who has done a few commercials and bit parts to go bananas and expect to come back to the party. There's forgiveness for true talent. Someone who's unknown, or moderately talented and they find out they have an addiction or some other type of challenge; they will never book them again. Either way, our behaviour, our choices, have repercussions. You can learn from them or not. It's up to you.

Tracey: Sure, because then you're just part of the problem, right?

Christina: Yup. I suppose it also depends on how much damage you do. Sometimes the ones that have only minor indiscretions never come back. I don't know what the formula is. There are always checks and balances in any actor's career, it's pretty unusual for them to not make a couple bad movies or have a couple quiet years. By the same token, there are always exceptions.

Tracey: Everybody does run up against these obstacles, unfortunately a lot of your profession is the fact that there's a lot of external forces at play. The biggest problem is that you've got somebody saying, at the end of the day, one person making a choice that can make a huge impact.

Christina: Actually, often it's too many people involved in making the decision that's the issue. Often I'm going into a room where they've already got an offer out. Where they're doing auditions in case their offers fall through. You can go to test at a network, and know that they're waiting to hear back whether or not some huge name is going to take it. I'm sure that Jessica Alba gets a couple of TV offers every year. Because they dream that big. You are never anybody's first choice. I don't mean it pessimistically; if you wrote a movie wouldn't you shoot for the moon? And they audition in case no one bites on the offers. And even then, there's a committee making the decision. It's just the reality of the process. You have everyone that's producing it, and then everyone at their studio that wants to have a hand in it, and then everyone at the network and on and on. When you go into a test, there can be 40 people there. So it's always casting by committee at that point.

What has kept Christina in the room for most of her adult life is the knowledge that she is being her authentic self and that those obstacles will eventually fall away. At the time of writing, Christina had just started filming a leading role on a major TV series during perhaps the worst downturn in the economy in recent history.

∞

Ville Valo has a surprisingly practical way to dissolve barriers – hard work.

Ville: The best way to prove it is to basically work and use the same tools as they do.

Tracey: Because that's what they respect. Success is what they respect. You know that people like Kat Von D., let's say... so many people look up to her now, and she's a huge success. But you know that if a person that looked like her but didn't have a TV show was walking down the street, there would be many comments. So she's got them where they respect her. As a person.

Ville: But at the same time you shouldn't be trying to validate yourself with success. Since only a tiny amount of people ever get that kind of success. And it's a combination of so many things, so it means that you just have to find that inner strength and when people try to push you down, you just fucking stand up again. It sounds stupid, but it is as basic as it is. If you come from a family with not necessarily as much money as the neighbors next door, it doesn't mean shit. It doesn't mean that their souls are well. It doesn't mean that their hearts are well. It doesn't mean that they're happy. And you know, I'm struggling for happiness with what I do. I'm not there, but it's been an incredibly interesting journey.

We can't all live in the space of Ernie Boch – where obstacles don't exist – all of the time. What's important to realize is that most obstacles are nowhere near as big or insurmountable as we give them credit for. They are simply what is – and nothing more. If we can acknowledge them with the same level of intensity that we notice the floor, a car, the sky, that they are simply part of existence and not imbued with some magical or special power, then they cease to be.

So take your fears, your worries and perhaps your far too in-depth knowledge of your challenges and dissolve them!

Chapter 12:
Being Authentic:
Without Navel Gazing

*"And if you gaze for long into an abyss, the abyss gazes
also into you."*

- Frederick Nietzsche

To thine own self be true. There isn't a self-help book on the planet that doesn't drive this point home, and this is no exception. We also recognize that many of us spend too much time wringing our hands trying to figure this out. If you're listening to your inner voice and being really honest about what it's saying, is it that difficult?

Melissa: I've been one of the hand wringers for a very long time. I've seen no less than three career counselors and they all say the same thing: you're musical, and you're creative. You should be writing or creating music or a combination of both. Well, as you can imagine, when you're trying to create a career in this world, those words can be a hell of a sentence. I've been at writing for some time now, with incremental success. Music? I let that go many years ago and I've only recently realized that I need it back in my life. Navel gazing? You bet. The only thing that has snapped me out of this recently is my pregnancy. All of a sudden it's not about me — and that's a good thing for someone obsessed with finding their "true self". Am I finished? Not yet, but all of a sudden there seem to be many more important things to focus on.

Mark Sanborn shared his feelings on being true to yourself.

Mark: I've always liked the quote that all progress is dependent upon unreasonable people. While being unreasonable can be an annoying personality trait, what I think the quote speaks to is that reasonable people have lower expectations, are willing to accept less and not willing to try quite as hard as the unreasonable man or woman. I'd like to think that has been part of my success. I've rarely been one to settle.

And Sloan Bella has dealt with the discomfort of knowing that being authentic sometimes makes those around her uneasy.

Sloan: When my stepson passed away, I knew that my stepdaughter would become pregnant and the spirit would be of her brother coming back again. And once again, I would blurt out this information and freak everyone out. It's like a form of psychic Tourette's. I can't help myself, that's the problem. I get around them and it's like, "oh God, this is going to happen, and this and this!" I do it with my friend's sons, when their nonsense is going on and they think that I'm neurotic and over protective and after it happens they'll call me and say " I can't believe that happened". And I'll say, it serves you right, because I warned you! It's like I'm jumping up and down saying "there's a brick wall, there's a brick wall!" And nobody listens to you. So I think in early childhood, when there's no fear of being ridiculed for who you are because you come in being ridiculed for who you are, you don't stay stuck in the idea of being worried about what other people think of you. You've already been told that you don't live up to the rest of your family, so in some sense it's a blessing. Because you're told that you'll never fit in. You're told that you're a zebra in a house of giraffes. Well, you're never going to fit in there so you just go about your life that way. You go about doing what you want to do. But I've never made choices based on logic and intellect, I've made them through my gut reaction, which can be a bit difficult. It's not logical. If I've seen it in a vision, I'll just get on a plane and move there. I won't have any backup, no money, no job, nothing. I completely live like that. That's not necessarily smart in this society, but it's worked for me.

∽

"Honesty" is the way to authenticity, offers Ville Valo:

Ville: I think whatever you do, you know this sounds stupid, but just fucking stay honest. If you want to make money, make money. If you want to play music, play music. And don't tell anybody otherwise. I hate double faced, mask wearing vultures. That's just a waste of everybody's time.

Tracey: Have you run into people like that in your career?

Ville: Uh, you know, sure I have. Many times, in the music business. You know, people try to give you advice on a musical level when their knowledge of music is based on the clang clang of the fucking bank teller. And that's fine, and you can listen to it, but you don't have to believe it. And so, honesty, perseverance and respect, because for those people in the business, and it's not an easy business, so for those people who are in there, they've done something right, and usually the thing they have done to sustain their careers is that they've never burned any bridges down, and that's something that a lot of people forget, especially when they get a bit of success.

Ville Valo performing during HIM's Venus Doom tour, 2007.
Photo by Danielle Batone Photography

Tracey: Yeah, they flip everybody off that's been on the path with them.

Ville: And you have to remember that it's a very small world, and it's even smaller in the entertainment world, and you never know who's going to be on top next week. So you don't have to suck up to people, or be overly sweet or saccharine, that's not the thing, it's just about the fact that occasionally people get there through sheer luck, but it's rarely. Most successful people have really worked their asses off to become who they are and where they are. You know, so those are the tips that I can give to people. We have to pledge our allegiance to the great old masters of rock and roll, and remember our roots, where it all comes from. I guess that's very important. At the same time, flip everybody off! *laughing* Tell them to just fuck off and believe in yourself and just go for it. And be blind and you know if somebody says "use the brakes, there's a wall in front of you", and you see the wall, just go for it.

Tracey: But aren't you contradicting yourself?

Ville: Yes, I am. I am. You gotta go with the flow, is what I'm saying. But I've been lucky, you know, I've met really, really nice people within the industry, and I've met not so really nice people as well, but if you meet people who you don't get along with, you don't hang out with them. And you just go the other direction. But you can still learn from them. Keep your friends close and you enemies closer, they said, back in the day. The "Art of War" is one of the best books that any freak can read.

Tracey: Really? I haven't read that one.

Ville: Well you should. It's the art of war, basically the philosophy of going into war, going into battle. And it's just classic, it's been quoted wherever...

Tracey: I've heard quotes, for sure...

Ville: A lot of it is bull...but it's still, you know, living your life as a freak, it is like going to war. And you do have to know your enemies, you know, the normal people...*laughs* know their ways.

Tracey: Now, I have a question; the most powerful song, to me off of Venus Doom (HIM's latest album) is Sleepwalking Past Hope. That song really grabbed me from the first time that I listened to the album. Actually, my son Alexander, that's his favorite song. And he asks me to put it on all the time.

Ville: Oh my God. He has a very macabre sense of music.

Tracey: He just loves that song. And I think that one has just a raw power behind it, and there is something about it that's very spiritual, and if you wanted to convey a powerful emotion with that song, you did it. Very strongly.

Ville: The only problem is that we don't know if it's the same one that we're talking about. *laughs* I don't know exactly what you felt.

Tracey: For me? Love and loss.

Ville: Oh my God. I feel confusion, and beautiful chaos. A blur. When you want to be, don't want to be, wanna do, and don't wanna do. Confusion between a lot of things, when you don't know what your heart tells you. And in that sense, it is love and loss.

Tracey: There's something very melancholy about it.

Ville: Well, it's very Scandinavian. And that's just the kind of music that I like to listen to. I don't like chirpie, chippery stuff… it's just not my cup of tea. When you're feeling light headed and all jokey, that's not when I'm listening to music. When I hang out with my friends at the local pub, fucking bullshitting and talking about the weather. In a very sado masochistic way, we make it as fun as possible. I don't know, all music is a double-edged sword; a blessing and a curse again. Blessed for the opportunity of expressing yourself in a way that you feel more whole with the universe and at the same time, cursed that you have to explain yourself to so many disbelievers.

Tracey: And have so many people ask you how you came up with the term "Love Metal", which is how your band's music is often described.

Ville: Oh, that too, that too. It's like you're given a bunch of keys to open a bunch of doors, and so you did just to find out that there's more doors behind them. So it's just the way we are. And bless the world for it. There is an opportunity let's say, you were saying that it's not mentally easy for a lot of people, but there are still people that do it, because they don't have an alternative. They go with the flow, and they have to do things, or they end up doing things for several reasons, and those people you can look up to. Iggy Pop and Blondie, and Baudelaire and whoever. Politicians and people who do what they believe in, that's erotic. That's a turn on.

Tracey: Absolutely. That lasts, it doesn't matter how old you are, it's still there. That honesty and authenticity.

Daemon and Raven Rowanchilde have a more "experimental" approach to the revelation of the authentic, rather than a destination in and of itself.

Daemon: I think that working, and not just work but using your intuitive process and just doing what you need to do is healthy. Rather than questing for your goals, you just need to look at it as more of an alchemical process instead of a pot of gold at the end of the rainbow. That's a very different process. Also, now I really feel a need to contribute or share something before I die. If I'm on my deathbed, I will feel more accomplished if there's something I've done that others can access or benefit from.

Tracey: Don't you think that Morpheus, Persephone, Faust, there's some elemental truth in it, that's a Universal Truth?

Raven: Yes, that it all boils down again to our free will. God's gift to us is the freedom to choose; that's a God gift, that's how we connect and create our reality. If we do it out of ignorance, then we're blown this way and that, or it seems like that, but if we do it with consciousness, then we can become the God creators of our own lives.

Tracey: Yes, when you operate with intention. And that gets back to "what you desire, desires you". There's that magnetic pull, because in some actuality, in some time frame you are actually making that happen. Going back to quantum physics, if all moments in time exist simultaneously, then you know that you are doing that somewhere out there, so you're striving to manifest it.

Raven: The marriage of spirit and flesh.

Tracey: That's right, and that's what aware people are trying to make happen.

∞

Bart Smit spends a great deal of his time trying to help his clients reach their true, authentic selves. Because he sees beyond the obvious, superficial manifestations of a person's composition, he's free to see the rawness of the soul.

Dr. Williams: You can't be happy when you have only created an outer reality. The outer reality is how we see ourselves and our identity. Unless we establish a deep connection with the inner realms, which sounds very new age, but in a sense, unless you start where you were created, how you are connected, what makes you breathe in this universe, if you cannot connect to the core of your identity, which is the inner self, what brought you into this world, your existence, the seed of where you derived from, then all of this will be endlessly meaningless. Until you get some kind of shift where you begin to understand the duality between the outer illusion and the inner self, because the outer illusion isn't real. It's just people playing out information and emotions, and that is an empty space. It isn't real. It is very important to be in the now. If you're not actually in the now, always two minutes from now, three minutes from now, five minutes from now, and if that's what we're doing, just riding the wave, then we're never going to have meaning, ever. It's not possible. We are simply adrenaline junkies, looking for the next ride, and it can be booze, drugs, emotions, whatever, to provide the adrenaline that the addict needs to cause that ride. It's not living in the now. It's chasing the dragon's tail, and that leads nowhere.

∞

So who are you, underneath all of the cloaks we all wear ever day? Who were you as a child? Has that changed much? Are you afraid or ashamed to accept the person you are at your core? Until you reconcile this first, basic relationship, authenticity is impossible.

Make it your project to identify who you are, what you want and then stop questioning that. Just be, then do the work you need to do to make it happen and you will have what you want.

Chapter 13:
Rebel With a Cause:
Knowing When to Rebel

"Let him that would move the world, first move himself."

– Socrates

When does being rebellious become a liability? And how does the Successful Rebel identify those battles worth fighting from those that simply diminish who we are by distracting us from the truth?

Artist Alex Grey shares his experience with successful rebellion:

Tracey: How have you managed to channel your rebellious nature so that it has helped you on your path to success? Do you have any advice for the other rebels out there?

Alex: I recommend meditation and a spiritual and creative life. Work on developing your centre and yourself. Make your intentions not just to be rebellious. Rebelliousness for its own sake is counter-productive. Rather, spend most of your time focused on doing what you love and what you know you do best. Useful rebellion would be to find a way to serve the world by bucking an outmoded or inefficient way of doing things. Investing personally in sustainable energy goes against the prevailing order, for example, but is essential for the survival of humanity.

Tracey: What else can you share with our Successful Rebels?

Alex: It is a fairly safe assumption that visionaries will maintain a stubborn adherence to inner guidance and question authority. Those traits have prevailed in my life along with demanding the absolute best of which I am capable in manifesting my own inspiration and creative insight. An unwillingness to accept easy answers or established forms and to be critical of my own work up to the moment of completion makes completing anything a challenge. Following these principles, an artist or entrepreneur meets with resistance, because they dare to be different and demanding of themselves and others. As we have moved into a community, others want to be heard and their concerns taken into consideration. As long as the necks of others are not at risk you can be an uncompromising rebel. When as a leader, your own name is on the line then so is your reputation and you have to be demanding of those that work with you and represent your mission.

Mark Sanborn shares his thoughts on living authentically:

Mark: "To thine own self be true" is good advice as long as one's own navel doesn't become the centre of the universe. We are rewarded in life in proportion to what we give, not what we get. That means that applying your best self (skill, strengths and passions) to the service of others will result in a very rewarding life. By the way, I've also observed that people often define "alternative" more on the basis of appearance than attitude or mindset. I'm certainly not going to be seen as an alternative person in terms of my appearance or lifestyle, but I think there are ways of thinking about business and life that I have that are alternative in the sense of being counter-cultural.

We agree Mark; it's not about the wardrobe.

∽

Sloan Bella runs a lot of her life on gut instincts, intuition and a deep knowledge that she knows who she is and what she wants.

Tracey: So, through your experiences, what advice would you give to someone that wants to do things on their own terms, but maybe avoid some of the pitfalls that you've encountered?

Sloan: Trust your instincts. Always. Even if it doesn't seem logical, I would say do it anyhow. Logic and success are not necessarily combined. I would say that, but I would also say to always protect yourself. You can integrate logical things. You don't have to reject every norm in society. Being a rebel doesn't mean that you have to be rebellious about everything, against any authority. Sometimes people in authority can be rebels as well, and they can have plenty of good ideas. You don't have to rebel against everything. It's not an all or nothing attitude.

Tracey: If you're a rebel, it doesn't mean that you have to rebel against things that are common sense. Things that can help you. You have to use the tools that are out there to advance yourself towards what you want.

Sloan: That's exactly right. It can be a stage of development as well. Think of a child. At some point they will go through a phase where no matter what you say to them, all they'll say back to you is "no!" They're not even listening to the logic. And rebellious people tend to do the same thing.

Tracey: And that's a major problem. The greatest success stories are usually rebels, but somehow they've reigned in that knee jerk reaction to rebel against everything. They channel their rebellion.

Sloan: They use it constructively, so they can creatively be unique. Or whatever they want. I would say that would be the one mistake that I've made. If anybody, a cop, a president, a doctor says something I feel like I have to argue with them! That's not a good thing! And also, I would say that I'm the biggest chicken and a fraidy cat. I'm a Leo, but I'm a scairdy cat. I'm like the cartoon whose hair stands on end and I run for the corner. I would say in the action of overriding your fear, it's more important to live your life. So in other words, if you're afraid of doing something because you're afraid that a, b and c will happen, you can still be afraid, but you have to take the action and do the fearful thing in order to progress your life. I've learned that, but that's been very difficult for me, because I'm afraid of pretty much my own shadow. For me, when I step on an airplane, I think I'm going to die. And then I'm like, you know what? Let's think of this as an adventure. Let's get on the airplane, you big stupid chicken, and then I get on the airplane.

Tracey: But maybe it's a healthy form of self-preservation, so you can't be too hard on yourself. You're better off being like that than overly reckless.

Sloan: For sure, but I've found that I can't allow myself not to do something because I have a ridiculous fear. So, I'm still afraid, but my actions are not. And that's a really important thing, to act like you're successful. The action of acting successful will attract that success to you. Visualizing, but more importantly acting. For example, if I'm a successful musician, for me to move forward I need to act as if I'm already that megastar that I want to be. I don't have to be drunk and crazy, but I can move forward in the action of taking myself seriously. People allow their ego to override their success. You know, worry about acting successful even when you aren't, the ego will try to stop you because it's worried about being judged. It doesn't matter!! People are always going to tell you that you can fail. You can count on that, so now you have to act as though you are going to be successful. And so, it's in that action that brings success. And the belief; even if you, in your mind are questioning yourself, it doesn't matter. Just the action of trying to believe, it stretches that muscle. Even if you don't believe it, you need to move forward. And the only thing that stops us is us. And that I've learned too. And the other thing that's important to remember, whether it's your parents trying to tell you what to do, or you telling your child, we are all on our own path and when you realize that, the need to control other people's actions is not as paramount, and the need to listen when they want to control yours stops as well. It's a very important step in our development as a person. When we accept that we are all on our own, on our individual learning path, it won't stress us out and distract us from our path.

Tracey: Right. Because you're so busy trying to backseat drive everybody else.

Sloan: Yes, it's craziness! Step back out of your own way, and everyone else's too. I don't presume to know God's plan for every single person in my family, just because they're in my family. I listened to it last night with a reading with a guy in jail, and he said that his son was in jail and he felt responsible, because nobody else in his family had been in jail prior to him. Where did that come from? He wasn't responsible for his son being in jail too, that was his son's own individual choice.

It was his path. We all have a path, and our individual choices lead us down it. No one else can take us there. Nothing happens to us that isn't relevant, and that's a hard pill to swallow. Especially when you're homeless and under a bridge. I believe that we have a lot of choice, especially in how we react to circumstances.

Chapter 14:
What's Your Definition of Success?

"Always bear in mind that your own resolution to succeed is more important than any other."

– Abraham Lincoln

Success means different things for different people. For some, it means a certain amount of material wealth, for others, a happy marriage, children or a thriving business. For many of us, fame seems to be the only definition of success; but there are so many wonderful, interesting ways to be successful.

Daemon and Raven Rowanchilde have what most people would consider a successful life – a thriving business, a happy home, peace and contentment in the country. How do they view success?

Tracey: What advice do you have for people who are trying to be successful, but wanting to do it on their own terms in their own individual way?

Daemon: The first thing that anyone needs to do is re-evaluate and investigate what success means to them.

Tracey: And that's where everybody says… "success, there's so many interpretations, and variables to success. Is it commercial success, or is it money, or is it being happy in your private life?" There are plenty of people who are rich and totally unhappy. So yeah, you have to find out what their idea of success is…

Daemon: Yeah, and what's important for you and not the things that you think you want because you're trying to please other people. What you value or appreciate. You have to do it for yourself. Others benefit out of it as well, of course, but you have to do it to express yourself.

Tracey: So when you got into being a tattoo artist, what was your prime motivation at the time? Did you say "this is what I want to be?"

Daemon: Yeah. I got a tattoo, I had an experience that I couldn't put into words. I was always pursuing art of some kind, and then I got a tattoo. Before that the only thing that I knew about tattoos was what I saw around, just your regular flash, nothing with any real depth and dimension, and what I thought had any meaning. When I got a tattoo, I saw the potential of the artwork and the experience as a transformative experience and that just opened up a doorway and I said "whoa... I have to do this."

Tracey: Did you feel a bit like you were just stepping onto a ride? Like you just buckled in and took off?

Daemon: It was like meeting a part of myself that I didn't realize that I had, and it just fit perfectly.

Tracey: So it was like finding a piece of the puzzle, a piece of your puzzle...

Daemon: And I didn't even know it was lost!

Tracey: Of course. And you're considered to be a very successful tattoo artist. A lot of them, for whatever reason, don't have it together... as much together business wise, stability wise...do you think that's because you guys are a couple? And you've got someone to help you with the business?

Daemon: Yeah, that's a very large part of it, and you have to be able to weather the storm, especially in the creative process...and having that backup and support, and of course the muse. An amusing muse! Sometimes you have to weather the storm, and part of the creative process is weathering the storm with Raven, however, you have to buckle yourselves up and close the shutters and the windows and then you start to get cabin fever, so it's a fine line...and then you have re-evaluate whatever you think that success is, or where you thought you were going and then you have to say, hold on, we've got it all wrong, we have to look at it all again, we have to change course, and then you have to go off in a totally different direction.

Tracey: Do you feel that you're a success, with the level that you're at now? What do you feel about where you're at now?

Daemon: I am successfully where I am at, and I am successfully moving beyond that every moment. So I'm successfully understanding more and more about who I am. So, I'm a success by many different standards, and I guess in certain frames of mind I could convince myself that I'm a failure. If I want to. But, yeah, I feel very successful. I don't get into all the things that I don't have, or play tricks on myself in my mind in that way. I am happy because I'm coming closer to myself, and that, for me, is very satisfying. And also, success means that I've let go of a lot of things that I used to think, which were baggage and bullshit. At different stages of my life, I thought that I had arrived, and I guess in some ways I might have, but really I hadn't. But in a lot of people's lives there are times when they think that things aren't going well, but they're right on the brink of success, and they give up just before.

We asked Neev how he defined success for himself.

Tracey: Now, you've just been through a big success, it's been covered in the media. Can you tell me a little bit about that, just so that I can give a bit of background on that?

Neev: Every year we run the Global Marijuana March, and there are two hundred cities in the world that celebrate that day on the first Saturday in May. The gathering in Toronto is the largest one in the world. So, when the weather's good, we have about thirty to forty thousand people that show up. It's to further the cause of legalization for medical or non-medical use.

Tracey: Within Canada, or within a larger scope?

Neev: Well, to be honest, it has an international scope, because drug policies in different countries all affect each other.

Tracey: Okay, so, with the successes that you've had with different cases within the Canadian court systems, and you've gone up against the big boys and won, what have your greatest successes been so far in what you're doing?

Neev: Well, it's hard to gauge. We're so far from our goal. We make small advances fairly regularly.

Tracey: Do you honor those as being successes?

Neev: I suppose, but there's so much more to do. We're winning these small battles, but there's no sense of winning the war.

Tracey: Do you have a clear picture in your mind as to what ultimate success is for Neev? Do you have a vision? What is the semi formed vision?

Neev: Well, where to begin? Legalized marijuana would change everything in my life. If it were like tobacco and alcohol, we wouldn't have to rely on organized crime. Or in the case of cannabis, disorganized crime. You would have legalized growers, and you would have an invoice, right? When something goes wrong, you would go to court. Right now there's no invoices and there's no courts. Tax it just like alcohol.

Tracey: You don't think that people would just be laying around stoned all day long? Little old ladies wouldn't be trading in their gin and tonic for the chronic?

Neev: No, I don't think it would change things that much.

∞

Ernie Boch's success isn't difficult to measure, based on external standards, but how does he see success?

Tracey: Well, after all the people that I've studied, you seem to be really blessed with the way that your life has played out with you being able to express yourself in that way, but I know so many people that have done well corporately, but for them to have ever done anything like you have would have been career suicide, you know what I mean?

Ernie: But I built up to it though. I purposely built up to it.

Tracey: What I want to do is have some kind of advice from you to give to people that want to express their individuality, but still be successful in business. What advice can you give them?

Ernie: Well, they have to have an overall plan. They can't just take it one step at a time; you have to have an end game. You have to sit in and say "if I do all this different stuff, what will it accomplish, and will it accomplish what I want?" About a year and a half ago, I did a spoof on the Coppertone tan ads, with the dog pulling down the bathing suit. That was my ass! That was my body doing that, I did that and we do stuff like that, but it's built up. I'm dressed as a total woman in the newspaper ads, and I'm a woman on TV. I have it now where it doesn't even phase people what I do. They're just "oh it's just Ernie being Ernie!" You know, and I purposely did that. I need to be able to do what I want, and people don't get freaked out, they think it's cool. They laugh with me.

Tracey: Sure, but what part of your attitude do you think has made that happen, because obviously there's something about you, your spirit or your personality that causes that openness in people, do you know what I'm saying? Because a lot of the time, somebody else who's not you would do something like that and they would be completely judged. So what is your magic that you've got with people? What tips can you give somebody that wants to create that same success?

Ernie: I think they've got to be comfortable in their own skin. They have to have an end game, they have to believe in what they're doing. You have to be confident enough to say, hey, I'm gonna do this and it's gonna be funny, it's gonna be good...a lot of times when I'm filming stuff, a lot of times I say to the people filming "look, it's gotta be funny, 'cause if it's not funny, it's gonna look sick, deranged, it won't be black humour, it'll just be dark, you know?"

Tracey: I know, and I love your black humour with your creature feature stuff that you do. I love that stuff.

Ernie: Yeah, that's cool, that stuff. I love it too.

In a professional landscape that is forever shifting, and you're only as good as your last project, how does an actor define success? We asked Christina Cox to share with us.

Christina: I think that you have to look at the markers of success for you, what does it mean to you? Is it financial stability? Is it doing Shakespeare in Central Park? Or is it being on the cover of US Weekly? What are your desires and motivations, because if you go to the root of some of them, they might not be that healthy. Maybe it's not working because it's your higher self protecting you.

Tracey: Yes, maybe it's completely ego driven.

Christina: That's definitely something that you're at risk of in the performing arts. The potential for ego stroking is just so high. And it can really get so "me, me, me". The reality is that part of the success of this job is financial security, so while I never really identified with the whole "million dollar bill" visualization, (I know that there isn't one, and I know that my agent isn't going to be handing me one.) But my agency will cut me a cheque when I get a job, and I know what the logo on the cheque looks like, so I use that for visualization. The reality is that I need to get paid. It's not completely for the art. You have to survive in the real world. It's just too easy to flounder and waste time. Aiming too high, letting your ego get in the way and then walking away from solid representation to sign somewhere prestigious but huge and impersonal is a common mistake driven by ego. If you find someone that passionately believes in your talent, and they're in a small agency, so what? Those one or two passionate people are so much better than twelve tepid ones. Persistence pays off, and I'd rather have that person out there trying to find an alternative route in for me if the main ones aren't working. You want someone who's passionate behind you. Don't worry if they're not a big name. Just get to work.

Tracey: How do you keep the faith when you're going through a patch where you have a gap?

Christina: You have to have other things to do. Other purposes in life.

Being in balance is a big part of it. If this matters too much, they can smell it on you, not to mention your whole life is on hold when you're not auditioning or working. It's an awfully big waste of time. And procrastination is epic in actors, because so much hangs on getting enough work before you go do a, b or c. You forget that your life is happening now. Then there's always this Murphy's Law phenomenon that happens when you finally do start something, (I started taking photography class at UCLA last year) and presto, you get a job. I had been sitting on my butt for three months, so I thought I'd take a class. But even though you know this is going to happen, that you'll get a job and have to quit, do it anyway. That always happens! It's the energy of progress, whatever kind, even if it's not in your field, it's going to move you forward. So I guess I'm saying I'd rather have to keep dropping things than be stuck sitting around waiting for the phone to ring.

Tracey: Sure. Action begets action. How important do you think it is to have some form of spiritual practice?

Christina: To be able to deal with all this? For me it's incredibly important. Because if I don't have a way of processing my experiences and my emotions, if I don't have a way of processing the disappointment and don't have a way of focusing my energy, it's really tough. I would rather continue to be sensitive and find ways through it, rather than getting detached but it can be hard. Whatever that process is, I think it's important to find it. If that's going for a run, if that's your meditation, if you can create flow that way, then do it. I'm not a card-carrying member of any specific doctrine, but meditation through movement has always helped me. Yoga, running, dancing, walking meditation. But I've had to laugh recently watching yoga become a competitive thing…like "oh, this is the yoga class that will get you shredded. You'll lose weight in this class." But if one person in that class finds a connection to some type of spirituality or grounding energy that helps them, great. Let the other twenty worry about their asses. Because that one person will have a ripple effect in their world. It's too bad that so much of it is so aesthetically focused, but I can't be too judgmental here because know that I was in a totally different place ten years ago, before I started exploring Buddhism and yogic philosophy among other things. It all helped me become a happier person.

Tracey: Yes, and of course everyone has moments of unhappiness, but at least now you can process it and deal with it.

Christina: Yeah! I mean, heck, Pema Chodron admits she sometimes gets mad in traffic. She's a Buddhist monk and writer and she's written some great books, but she gets angry sometimes too. We're all human, and it's not about being above feelings. It's not about finding a way to not feel. And you also have to be aware that what you're manifesting is not negatively worded or framed. You can dwell on the negative too much, and then it just snowballs. You have to frame it another way. Words are incredibly powerful. You can't say, "I don't want" a bad employee or " I don't want to be in debt" or whatever your worry is, because all the Universe hears is "bad employee" and "debt", not the qualifier. You have to be careful of that. What comes out of your mouth most often is what you create. I personally have to be really careful. There's a fine line between expressing your displeasure or disappointment with certain situations, and making it real. I didn't get a show I really wanted, and I was venting about it to a friend and she called me on it, so I still have to watch myself when I do that, because I don't want to re-enforce or manifest that disappointment any more than necessary in my life. It just attracts more of the same.

Tracey: Yes, it's all about "like attracts like" and "As above, so below."

Christina: That's the tricky one, and the thing that takes the most work is shifting out of that negative place. Out of grief or sadness or loss or fear. Fear is a huge one to get over. Clear out that stuff from your heart because it will doom you. But it's hard work. I'm trying to do that right now. It's an ongoing process. Constant vigilance.

By most people's standards, Ville Valo and his group HIM are considered successful, with a fan base of millions worldwide. "Success" appears to be something he's not entirely comfortable bestowing upon himself.

Tracey: What is success to you?

Ville: Success for me means being a success in life, which equals happiness, and I'm not happy. You have moments of enjoyment, but that's very far from happiness. And fulfillment in happiness. Where your heart is full and you feel safe. Then, at the end of the day, the struggle to get there is again, interesting and worth many more stories than the actual blissful existence. So, it's kind of like a double-edged sword when it comes to that. And you know success, I do have a roof on top of my head, I do have a can of Coke, and I do have my fags... meaning cigarettes.

Tracey: Yeah, we're familiar with that term here.

Ville: Anyways, you know that a song can be a success, but it doesn't mean that the person is a success. A song is so many different moving parts, and getting a song successful means getting people that believe in it, in the business side of things and people who want to feed it to the radio, and people who want to listen to it, and call the radio stations up, you know there's so many variables that don't have anything to do with the person who actually made the song. So I think that in that sense, that a song or a piece of art, it does live its own life, and the more successful it is, you know...everyone that's seen the Mona Lisa is basically a part of its success story in a way. Making it more successful.

Tracey: Sure, and I mean, look at the Heartagram. (The Heartagram is an intertwined heart and pentagram, designed by Ville Valo as the symbol for HIM) It's a life form on its own. It's got its own life.

Ville: Yeah, and I'm happy for it. It's like a metaphysical kid. It's just something that I drew down and I didn't want to be really strict with it. You know, I have it trademarked and everything, but I like to see it go where it goes. And I don't know what it means. I have my own ideas occasionally, but I am as right or as wrong as a person who's listening to, let's say, a song of mine. Their interpretation of a lyric is as valid as mine.

Sloan Bella is well known in the field of psychics and seers, spending enough time in the spotlight and working with police forces to feel successful on a number of fronts.

Tracey: Your gift brought you tons of torment as you grew up, but it's what brought you your success now. You never would have been a regular on the Montel show. And what other shows are you doing right now?

Sloan: Many. One for Canadian TV, oddly enough. I just put a pilot together for that, and A and E, I'm doing a show for them looking for the missing billionaire adventurer, Steve Fawcett, so I just shot that. Looking for him with his biographer. So I do a lot of things, a lot of psychic TV shows. I always wanted to do TV, and always wanted to do it psychically. I never wanted to be an actress. I want to intuitively perform, I don't want to act somebody else's words. I always knew that, so I had great success as soon as I moved to LA. And I don't mean that I'm particularly famous, I just mean that I worked consistently for twenty years doing psychic TV, which is fine for me.

Tracey: So that's what you set out to do. And if you look at the definition of success in the dictionary, it's the achievement of something desired, planned or attempted. So obviously, that's what you wanted and that's what you got.

Sloan: Yes, that's exactly what I got. I was able to live a life that is good for me, even though plenty of people have called me crazy or a crackpot, or whatever. But you get that in any occupation or walk of life.

∞

Bill Jamieson has had one of the most interesting and varied careers we've ever encountered. Does he consider himself a success?

Bill: I am a really good salesman. I have the gift of the gab and I work very hard so I've always been successful at work, from aluminum siding sales to contracting. By the time I was forty years old, I had run my own construction companies for more than fifteen years and was considered to be a success. I had money, nice cars, and was engaged to be married to a beautiful woman, but it felt like I had been working on an assembly line - successful but unfulfilled. Then I had a surprising spiritual experience, which I can't really explain, but I realized that I lacked passion in my life and had to search for it. This is what led me to my travels in Ecuador and Peru. I found an anthropologist from New York named Daniel who was living in Iquito, Peru. He was interested in natural healing and at the time I was researching a drug used by certain cultures for healing called ayahuasca. I headed down to Iquito, Peru with a couple friends and met up with Daniel. I ended up doing ayahuasca for the first time with a Spanish Shaman just outside of Iquitos. It was a very interesting experience. Then we rented a boat to go down the Amazon River to visit the Shuar Tribe. Sadly, it was a dry time of year and we could not get to the area. I went back to Toronto, and planned my second trip. This time I flew to Quito, Ecuador and left from there to Macus, into the Ecuadorian jungle. Eventually we reached a Shuar village where I met an Elder Shuar Shaman named Tukupi. He let me sit in on traditional healing ceremonies where he was using ayahuasca and, with his guidance, I ended up having one of the visions that led me to what I am doing today. I returned to visit Tukupi on three separate occasions, twice with Daniel, and once on my own. In the process I began to learn quite a bit about the Shuar people and their customs. At the time I was in the construction and waterproofing business. I found a shrunken head for sale, but sadly it was in the ten thousand dollar area. I decided to try to put an ad in the Toronto Star "Wanted: Authentic shrunken head". They would not allow me to put it in. I then contacted the Globe & Mail, our national newspaper, and they let me put in an ad, but I had changed it to "Collector seeks authentic shrunken heads". I managed to purchase three shrunken heads within thirty days. This lead to my interest in different cultures and customs from around the world. I had found my passion, and the ad is still in the Globe today, but now has expanded to Ancient and Tribal Artifacts. I started attending tribal art fairs and following auctions, as well as collecting books on many cultures from around the world. Although not an academic, I enjoyed my research.

In 1999, my girlfriend and I decided to take a Sunday drive to Niagara Falls. I had quite a large collection of shrunken heads at the time, and I took her to Niagara Falls to see Ripley's Believe it or Not. I also took her to the Niagara Falls Museum. It contained Egyptian mummies, a 40 foot humpback whale skeleton, hundreds of North American Indian artifacts, antique guns and other weaponry from around the world, and panoramic exhibits of taxidermy contained on four floors. After touring the museum, I met the owner, Jacob Sherman whose grandfather purchased the museum on the 1940's. He was the third generation owner and ran the museum with his wife. I introduced myself to Jacob and asked if he would be interested in trading some Indian artifacts for shrunken heads, as Ripley's up the street had shrunken heads, and he had none. As I was walking out of the museum, and I don't know why, but I turned and said to Jacob "Have you ever thought of selling the place?". He replied, "Make me an offer." The next day I got in touch with my lawyer and began researching the value of the building. So did Jacob Sherman. The value of the real estate, having a view of Niagara Falls on the fourth floor was way beyond anything I could afford or beyond anything Jacob Sherman could have imagined. I believe that no one had looked at the value of the property since the 1970's. I did not even realize that there was a park beside the museum that was also part of the museum property. Selling the property was not going to be a problem. Jacob and his wife worked long hours to keep the museum running, and when the appraisal came in, it made much more sense to sell the property. But what about all the contents? It was the last cabinet of curiosity left of its type in North America. Jacob and I started to negotiate the purchase of the Museum and contents. We had five experts from Sotheby's fly in to appraise the contents of the museum. The appraisal for nine Egyptian coffins and nine Egyptian mummies was in the $175 thousand to $250 thousand dollar range. Sotheby's put an appraisal together for us for what they felt the contents of the museum were worth. I felt the collection my Egyptian mummies were at least worth a minimum of two million dollars. All of the experts thought I was crazy. Jacob wanted more than double that of the appraised value for the museum. I really believed that there was a museum somewhere in the world that did not have an Egyptian mummy collection, and mummies sell tickets. I came to a deal with Jacob, and paid him a non-refundable deposit for the amount he wanted for the museum name and contents and set a closing date. Gayle Gibson, an Egyptologist from the Royal Ontario Museum in

Toronto had studied these mummies and written a report on them a few years before. I obtained a copy of the report and brought her on as a consultant. She had felt that one of the mummies had Pharaoh like qualities. I had a good friend and photographer, Marty MacDougall photograph the entire collection. With Gayle doing the text, and Marty designing and putting a website together, which is still up today www. egyptianmuseum.com, we acquired a museum directory; a list of all museums around the world. Any museum that exhibited antiquities of any kind got a letter directing them to the website offering the complete collection for sale. Within a period of two weeks, we had several museums interested in one or two mummies, and three major museums interested in the complete collection. The first museum to fly in to look at the collection was the Michael C. Carlos Museum of Atlanta, Georgia, and then there was interest from the Smithsonian, and the Edinburgh Museum, Scotland. With these other institutions wanting to come see the mummies with serious interest in purchasing the collection, Atlanta agreed to put a $200,000 dollar deposit on the collection and the balance paid shortly after. They then went on to raise the money. This helped me pay for the purchase of the museum, and gave me a substantial inventory to become a dealer in Ancient and Tribal Art. The mummy with the crossed arms turned out to be the missing Pharaoh, Ramses I. Atlanta had suspected this and caused them to move swiftly. I'm not the person who discovered Ramses I, but the person who sold him. The credit goes to the Egyptologist from the Michael C. Carlos Museum. Why would I go to Niagara Falls that day? Why did I offer to buy the museum, why would I offer to pay double the appraised value for the contents of the museum? Why did I believe that the mummies were worth over two million dollars? I don't know. Maybe the stars lined up in my favor, or perhaps I was just a salesman that was going to be the catalyst that started the wheels in motion for Pharaoh Ramses I to return back to Egypt. The Niagara Falls Museum contained many historical treasures from around the world that had never been studied or even known to have existed. This launched my career as a dealer in the Ancient and Tribal art world. You ask if consider myself a success? I'm not done yet, but it feels like I am on the right path. I am doing what I truly want to be doing with my life I am still finding treasures and will continue to do so until the day I die.

Tracey: Tell me about one of your recent discoveries.

Bill: I was in New York with my friend, Henry Galliano, who is a paleontologist and owns a shop called Maxilla and Mandible. He is very involved in the excavation and selling of dinosaurs and other natural history specimens. About five years ago, we went to an auction in New York that was selling dinosaurs. This was where I first laid eyes on this skull that looked like a dragon, as though when alive it could breathe fire. The head has devil horns that run all the way down the top of its head to its nose. It was a new species of dinosaur, and this head was the only one that was found on the planet by a ranch-hand in the Dakotas. These dinosaurs are over sixty million years old and the skull is all that remains because the bone was like armor. The rest of the skeleton disintegrated. I really love the look of this creature. I wanted to buy it but the price was too high. It ended up being purchased and donated to the Children's Museum of Indianapolis, where it was given the name Dracorex hogwartsia, in honor of the Harry Potter series. I asked my friend Henry to let me know if he ever hears about another one and, low and behold, last year Henry called with the news. Another skull has been discovered in the Dakotas. I contacted the owners and put a deposit on the head. Currently, the head is in pieces, and much of it still incased in rock. However, this specimen is more complete than the Indianapolis one, and it has a bottom jaw. My friend, Sheldon Jafine, and I have purchased the skull, and we will be loaning it to the Royal Ontario Museum's (ROM) paleontology department. They are going to restore it, assemble it and put it on permanent exhibit. The great thing about this is that this is the second Dracorex to be discovered, and hopefully in a year or two you will be able to go there and visit it. Under the on loan sign, the dedication will be to Angus Young and AC/DC. This is called having fun with museum donations!

Tracey: So, if you could give some advice to a rebel that wanted to be a success, what would be the number one piece of advice that you would offer?

Bill: Never give up. Don't be afraid to ask for help and keep searching until you find the answer; the great thing about the world and the internet today, is that if you find a book, and the author is still alive, you can usually get in touch with them. It's also very important to remember that you can change careers and reinvent yourself no matter how old you are. When people say no, or that you can't, use what they say as strength to prove them wrong. I opened a fortune cookie some time ago, and I keep the paper taped on my computer screen. It reads, "Only one who attempts the absurd can achieve the impossible".

How do you define success? Our interviewees have defined it as broadly as happiness, a feeling of calm, helping others, selling tickets or even selling mummies! What's important is how you see success.

If success for you is being able to go your own way while paying your bills and staying true to yourself, awesome! If it's standing up and performing in front of 50,000 people in a stadium, great! Sell twenty cars this week? That's equally valid. What's important is that you are coming from a place of authenticity, that you're operating from your highest self.

Tracey: One of the most important success tips that I have discovered over the course of my life is to make sure that you practice "constructive daydreaming" instead of "destructive daydreaming". You can find this concept in many sports psychology texts. Focus your mind on visualizing what you want right before bed and right before you get out of bed, when the subconscious has been proven to be more receptive. Any other time during the day when you see yourself thinking negative thoughts or the worst-case scenario, try to turn it around. Daydream about good things happening, the best-case scenario, and your dreams coming true. It's really easy to let your mind go down the dark path, but try and catch yourself when you do and turn the thought around. Make it a game if you need to. Remember when you were a kid and dreamt about being a rock star, with thousands of screaming fans? Do that again. If you do, I guarantee that your life will change for the better. Most of the problems with the world today are caused by people operating out of fear. Don't be one of them. Master your thoughts.

Make sure to keep a journal of your goals, hopes and dreams. Accepted wisdom has shown that if you address your requests to whatever higher power you respect (the Universe, God, the Angels, Buddha, Krishna, the Goddess, Ozzy Osbourne, whatever) and write them down, your chances of them manifesting are much higher than leaving them as some half formed desire. Ask for what you want! Try to state the request in the present tense and give thanks for it showing up in your life. Don't forget to say thank you! An "attitude of gratitude" will always open you up for more blessings. Let's put it this way. If you gave a lovely gift to someone and they neglected to say thank you, would you want to make that effort again? Very doubtful. The same is true for the Universe. It will avoid giving gifts to those that forget to be grateful. To get the ball rolling, start today by giving thanks for everything good in your life. Even if things are really tough, there will be something to be grateful for. This will set you up to receive more good things, as everyone likes to be acknowledged for giving, even the Universe. Give credit where credit is due, and your connection with the Universal Truth will increase.

Tracey: I have personally experienced how very powerful journal writing can be. Sometimes it can take many years for your dreams to manifest, so make sure to keep your journals and look through them every once in awhile. The things that actually happen because you set the ball in motion by sending out a request to the Universe can be mind blowing. This is kind of a silly example, but it still amazed me when it happened.

One of the first albums that I ever bought was Led Zeppelin Four. I bought the album when I was eleven years old, and promptly fell in love with Robert Plant. That voice, that face, the hair....I was mesmerized, and one evening I wrote in my diary "One day, I'm going to kiss Robert Plant". Fast-forward thirty years. My husband took me to see Robert Plant play here in Toronto a couple of years ago, and we managed to secure VIP tickets, which had access to the backstage area. We were sitting having a drink when someone shouted "Robert Plant's here!" I glanced across the room and saw this tall, still handsome rock God trying to peel a woman off of his neck. She wouldn't let go, and it was pretty comical to watch him trying to make his getaway. His bodyguard finally got the woman off, and as he was hastily making his exit, I jumped out of my chair and called "Robert, will

you sign a copy of your new cd for me?" I had just bought a copy of his new album, and it was sitting in my purse.

The smile that came over his face was like the sun coming out of the clouds. He walked back across the room, scooped me up and gave me a huge kiss and hug. And it was a long hug! My face was mashed into the side of his neck and that famous hair, and all I could think was that the goal that I had set as a twelve year old girl had come true, except he had kissed me, not the other way around! After he had hugged me, he held me at arm's length, looked into my eyes and said "Do you have a pen?" We both burst out laughing. I didn't have a pen, as I had not anticipated this gift from the Universe to drop into my lap like this. Robert sent his bodyguard to get a sharpie, and we chatted as he signed my copy of Mighty Rearranger. After he said goodbye, I turned around and apologized to my husband for kissing another man. He laughed at me and just said "It was Robert Plant! How could I be mad at that?"

I think that this story demonstrates two principles of success, actually. The most obvious is, of course, the importance of goal setting and writing down your hopes and dreams. But there was also another lesson in this encounter for me. Showing interest in others is a powerful thing. Because I had shown interest in Robert Plant's current career (buying the new album), he went out of his way for me. People appreciate when you have genuine interest in them. The other girl that was just blindly trying to kiss him was simply peeled off by a bodyguard, because she was only interested in one thing, and it certainly wasn't his current musical interests. Go the extra mile to show interest in others, and really listen to them as well. Don't just wait for them to finish speaking so that you can talk! I run into that attitude all the time in business, and it is a complete and utter turn off. Some jerk simply waiting for me to finish speaking so that he can talk will never get the big business deal, the big payoff, or sell me anything. I'll just barely tolerate them, and then get away from them as fast as I possibly can. I think that this is true of most people, so keep it in mind. Slow down. Enjoy the ride.

A famous celebrity marketer has been quoted as observing that he and pretty much all successful people are obsessed with the relentless pursuit of "more". We don't think that is true of every Successful Rebel, but we do think that it can be difficult for successful people to actually feel that they are a success. Many of the people that we approached to speak with us have had great success, but still don't feel successful because they know that there is so much more out there for them to do, to be, or to achieve. It's easy to allow this to make you unhappy if you dwell on it, but we think that the desire for "more" is there to spur you on, not bog you down or make you obsessive. Desire is there as a guide, a beacon. Follow it with a pure heart and eventually you will have what your heart desires. Don't give up. The only way that we truly fail is by giving up. The journey is the spirit and driving force of success. Embrace it!

One of the strange misconceptions about success that we encountered in our research is people's perception that success is some kind of mythical destination in life where finally you have everything that you want and things are perfect. In fact, we had a few people that we wanted to interview decline because even though they have had massive success in their lives, they were going through a rough patch, and therefore didn't feel that they had anything to offer in the way of advice or knowledge for others. Nothing could be further from the truth! Difficult times happen in every life, and if we can learn from others how to deal when the shit hits the fan, then maybe we can feel better equipped to deal with our problems and not feel so alone. The anonymous quote "Pain and suffering is inevitable, but misery is optional" kind of sums it up. We all need to remember that it's okay to be vulnerable, it's okay to be sad and admit that we don't have all the answers. The true crime is not being authentic with others and especially yourself. Lying about your feelings and presenting a false face to the world causes most of the problems that we encounter in our day-to-day life. If we could only admit that we don't have all the answers, that we're not perfect and that sometimes we all need help, our health and happiness would take a quantum leap forward in a life of authenticity. Be the rebel! Be honest in the face of falsehood, and your true destiny will step forward to hold you up in times of struggle.

We are entering into a time of unprecedented upheaval, growth and opportunity for everyone to take a look at what they're doing and decide if it's working for them, and for the world. As we wrapped up the first draft of this book, Barack Obama was being inaugurated as the first African American president of the United States.

The world is ripe for change, the world needs and is demanding that we all take responsibility for who we are and contribute our unique gifts. There has never been a better time to seize your freedom, cast off the shackles of conformity and claim your place in the world.

The rise of the Successful Rebel is now!

Here is The Successful Rebel's cheat sheet:

1. Identify the trait that brought you torment as a child – it's likely what made you unique.

2. Develop a built-in bullshit detector.

3. Don't sell yourself out – the deal with the devil is never worth it.

4. Find moments of bliss in what you do – or do something else.

5. Quiet your mind with non-destructive modes of relaxation.

6. Understand that this won't be easy – and don't expect it to be.

7. Work your ass off.

8. Don't be put off by the down times – everyone has them.

9. Martyrdom is overrated – so get off the cross.

10. Deal with your enemies with resolve, but with love.

11. Don't take no for an answer.

12. Know yourself, but don't get stuck navel gazing.

13. Rebel when it makes sense, not for the sake of rebellion.

14. Succeed by your own standards.

MORE SUCCESSFUL REBELS

Shortly after we wrapped the first draft of this book and started to speak with others about the concept of the Successful Rebel, an interesting thing happened. More and more people wanted to talk to us: successful, unusual, creative people who wanted to share their life experiences. Even more interesting, the vast majority of the people that came into our lives at this time were women!

Hence the idea of the Successful Female Rebel was born. In our next book, we'll be focusing on the trailblazing women that have struck out on their own and done something truly amazing.

For a sneak peek at our next book, please meet Ariellah.

Ariellah is considered a superstar of belly dance, and performs for enthusiastic audiences all over the world. Ariellah studied classical ballet extensively with the Royal Academy of Dance of London for twelve years, beginning at age three. After a break from dance that included graduating from UC Davis and two years in the Peace Corps on Africa's Ivory Coast, she returned to the United States eager to learn the dance of her Moroccan ancestry. Ariellah's style reflects and infuses her personal interpretation of Middle Eastern belly dance, with a modern, dark flavour, that is uniquely her own. She is widely known for her strong stage presence and unrivaled technique. Her performances are designed to mesmerize and invoke emotion and the darker, more passionate side of dance. Ariellah believes her style emanates from the passion and contentment that belly dance has brought to her life, as well as the infusion of her lifelong involvement in the gothic subculture, allowing her to fully express herself in a unique and beautifully dark way. For more information on Ariellah, go to ariellah.com.

Ariellah. Photo by Sequoia Emmanuelle

Tracey: One of the things that I've noticed in all of the successful rebels that I've interviewed is that the character trait that brought them the most torment as they grew up was actually the key to their success later on in life.

Ariellah: For sure. That is so interesting, immediately my mind goes to remembering as a kid, yeah I had some family stuff, but in terms of other kids at school, you know not being accepted and really being taunted and being made to feel like an outcast, it made me feel bad about myself. I definitely brought that into my teaching. I know how it feels to be really shy, and to not feel good about myself and to have people not be nice to me, so I think that it's made me be overly compassionate to each student that I meet and each dancer. And I receive emails and personal feedback from all of these people all over the world, basically saying "thank you for taking the time to talk to me, and making me feel comfortable". I think I brought that with me, does that make sense?

Tracey: Absolutely. And that's a key component of your teaching, obviously, because you have to let them be relaxed about themselves and their bodies too, right?

Ariellah: In some ways it's almost like a motivational speaker. I'm kind of like that in my workshops and it's really caught on, in that the response is overwhelming. People want me to come and teach and teach and teach, because apparently, some other instructors may not be as in tune with the dancers that they are teaching. I think that's really benefited me well in terms of just being a really nice, good teacher. Giving people self-confidence instead of being, you know, why is your body doing that? I take this very soft, encouraging approach as opposed to being judgmental and sticking my nose in the air.

Tracey: Sure. And I would think that the students would be very intimidated because to do belly dancing you're really putting yourself out there. And a lot of we woman are not this perfect size two and all that kind of garbage.

Ariellah: Totally. And you know, it's actually better with belly dance to have more size. And the funny thing is that a lot of students come because they think that belly dance looks so easy and they find that, my God, the muscle isolation is out of control! People get discouraged and frustrated, and I really try to impart my knowledge with my own experiences where I've had the frustrating times but I knew that I could do it. So I try to get across that they can do it too, through drilling, through constant practicing and I try to keep them motivated though telling my own story.

To read Ariellah's full story, and those of other amazing female Successful Rebels, check our website thesuccessfulrebel.com for updates.

About the Authors

Tracey Cox is the General Manager of an established and well respected new car dealership and sits on the board of directors of a multimillion-dollar automotive corporation. She is also a writer and avid student of success. This is her first book.

Melissa Ireland was trained as a writer at UCLA's prestigious screenwriting school and later attended the Canadian Film Centre, where she penned the short film "Bridal Path". She now spends her time running a bustling local news website and has moved to non-fiction writing.

If you would like to join our growing community of Successful Rebels, please visit our website at www.thesuccessfulrebel.com.

Contact Us

To reach us, or to book Tracey Cox and Melissa Ireland for speaking engagements, please visit www.successfulrebel.com, or mail us at:

Successful Rebel

260 Adelaide St. E

Suite 66

Toronto, ON

M5A 1N1